Feeder Fishing
For
Carp, Bream and Roach

By
Richard Blackburn

Copyright © 2022 Richard Blackburn
All rights reserved

ISBN: 978-1-8382478-4-3

Table of Contents

Foreword..11
Feeder fishing...13
Equipment...14
   Rods..14
   Rough guide to rod choice..16
   Reels for feeder fishing..18
      Fishing reel gear ratio...19
      Wide spool reels..20
   Fishing reel main lines...20
      Line strengths and diameters....................................22
   Balanced tackle..23
   Rod rests and setup on the bank....................................24
      Backrest..25
      Rod position...25
Basic skills..26
   Casting a feeder...26
      Setup to cast..26
      Line drop..27
      Prepare to cast...27
      Swing and cast...27
      Accuracy of direction..28
      Setting casting distance..29
      Casting to the line clip and landing the feeder............31
      Casting unclipped and landing the feeder.................32
      The feeder has landed...33
   Plumbing the depth with a bomb...................................34
Flatbed feeders..35
   Inline flatbed feeders..36
      Setting up an inline feeder..37
      Hook links..39
      Hooks for flatbed feeders..39
      Tying a hook link...41

- Knotless knot - hair rig..42
- Pellet band..42
- Quick stop..46
- Bait bayonet..47
- Baits to use with a flatbed feeder.....................................48
  - Hookbaits..48
    - Hard pellets..48
    - Hookers (soft pellets)...49
    - Expanders..49
    - Boilies...50
    - Wafters..50
    - Pop-ups..51
    - Boosters, liquids and sprays...................................51
  - Feed baits...52
    - Preparing pellets..53
    - Dampening pellets..53
    - Groundbait...54
    - Mixing groundbait..55
- Hybrid and Banjo feeders..56
  - Rigs for Hybrid and Banjo feeders.................................57
    - Preparing pellets..59
    - Loading a Hybrid feeder..59
    - Loading a Banjo feeder...61
    - Hookbait - part of the trap....................................61
  - Fishing the Hybrid..64
    - One fish at a time...65
    - Best Hybrid waters...66
    - Hybrid/Banjo techniques..67
    - Bites and indications..69
  - Method feeder...70
    - Using a Method feeder..71
    - Preparing the feed...71
    - Loading a Method feeder..72
    - Feed too wet...73
    - Feeding approach...74
    - Winter Method feeder fishing...................................76

Quick change feeders..76
Hook baits..79
Pellet feeders...79
How pellet feeders work..80
Preparing the pellets...80
Loading a pellet feeder...81
Using a pellet feeder..81
Open End Feeders..83
Rods and reels...84
Fishing line..85
Essential rigs..87
The running rig...88
Keep it simple...88
Tying the basic running rig..89
How the running rig works..91
Running rig bites...92
When and where to use the running rig.......................94
The feeder link running rig...96
Tying the feeder link running rig......................................97
Using the feeder link running rig......................................97
Which rig to use..98
The Helicopter rig..101
Tying the Helicopter rig..101
Using the Helicopter rig..103
Helicopter rig bites..103
Other rigs..104
Hook links (hooklengths) for all rigs.............................105
Feeders..108
Four essential feeders..110
Plastic feeder - open end feeder....................................110
Cage feeder...111
Maggot feeder...112
Rocket feeders..113
Feeder fishing baits..114
Groundbaits...115
Bream groundbait..115

- Roach groundbait..116
- Preparing groundbait for Bream or Roach................117
- Preparing particles..118
- Loading a feeder..118
- Stillwater feeder fishing..120
  - A practical approach..121
    - Setup for two swims...122
    - Rods and tips...124
    - Quiver tips..124
  - Feeding approach...128
    - Cold days...130
    - Mild days...132
    - Hot days..136
  - River feeder fishing..138
    - River setup...138
    - Feeder weight and quiver tips..................................139
    - Fishing the bow..140
    - Keep it simple on a river..142
    - Maggot feeder...143
    - Bread...143
  - List of feeders..145
    - Plastic open end feeder..145
    - Cage feeder..146
    - Rocket feeder..147
    - Maggot feeder...148
    - Dome feeder..149
    - Bell feeder...150
    - Window feeder...151
    - Finned feeder..152
  - Further thoughts..153

Foreword

Float fishing a river is how I started out in angling, cycling out into the Sussex countryside to fish the free stretch of the river Adur. At that time, the only other method I was aware of was ledgering. A method that seemed to me to be a bit hit and miss.

I didn't know of the revolution soon to come, the evolution from ledgering to a method that could put feed and hook bait close together time after time.

Feeder fishing exploded onto the match scene much to the disgust of traditionalists, but it was such a successful variation of ledgering, it quickly spread throughout angling.

This book is about feeder fishing for Carp, Bream and Roach only. It covers feeder fishing techniques for still and running water in a clear practical way. I have assumed you have some angling experience to save time in explaining the basics.

Best of luck with your fishing, Richard.

Feeder fishing

A well established principle in fishing is to attract the fish to an area with free offerings. Just as you might scatter bread on your lawn to attract birds, throwing some feed in the water will attract some fish.

Feeders can be fished well beyond the range of throwing groundbait or catapulting loose feed. With a feeder, the hookbait can be presented close to the feed every time and at a greater distance. Feeders put the feed right where it's needed, next to the hook bait, whether fishing a river or lake.

Most anglers understand the idea of feeding the fish, but don't realise it applies to feeder fishing too. I often see people taking time and patience to prepare some feed to use, but then do not use it to it's full advantage. Feeders are not just a one fish at a time trap, a feeding strategy must be adopted to keep the fish coming. After location, how an angler feeds the fish has the most impact on how well the session goes.

The author playing a Carp caught on a Method feeder.

Equipment
Rods

To get the most from a feeder rod, a balance between rod, reel, line, distance cast and to a degree, tip strength must be struck. Unlike float fishing where the target species is the starting point which leads to line strength and so to rod and reel choice. Casting distance is the first factor in deciding which rod and reel to use when feeder fishing. Many purpose built commercial fisheries are designed to make life as easy as possible for the angler. Their waters frequently feature an island within comfortable casting range, the banks of which are natural holding areas for Carp. On the other hand, a reservoir presents the angler with acres of open water where a long cast may be needed to reach the fish. Clearly a more powerful rod and a heavy feeder is needed to make a long distance cast, as opposed to a short chuck to an island.

Casting distance in my opinion is the main consideration for selecting the correct rod for still water. Once a line or feature has been identified, the distance to that spot will indicate the power of the rod needed. As a rough guide, one metre of distance will require 1 gram of casting weight to reach. A 30m cast should be easily achieved with a 30g feeder, therefore a rod rated to cast 30g should do the job. Manufacturers usually suggest a range of weights any particular rod is designed to cast. The suggested maximum and minimum casting weight are just that, the least and the most, but not the ideal weight to cast.

A rod may have a maximum casting weight, but I have found the optimum casting weight is usually around 70 to 80 percent of the maximum stated. That's not to say the rod cannot cast it's maximum rated weight, but that generally I find is the rod loads and launches a feeder better, if it's casting a little less than it's stated maximum.

The length of a feeder rod follows the casting weight. Short rods cast low weights a short distance. Long rods cast heavy weights long distance. Under normal circumstances the length of the rod is not an issue, as there is little choice other than to use progressively longer rods to cast further and further away.

Casting distances are usually less on a river, but a heavy feeder may be needed to hold the bottom. The casting weight of the rod remains the main guide to rod choice, but on a river, flow rather than range is the deciding factor.

An ideal action for a long powerful feeder rod is a very progressive, almost tippy action. The top third should be flexible enough to play small fish without bumping them off the hook. The much stiffer midsection takes the strain to play the bigger powerful fish. Distance feeder rods need to be two rods in one, a soft top section with a strong back bone for landing hard fighting fish.

As the range lessens and the rods get shorter, the action of the rod changes. At very close range, short rods called, "Wands" or "pickers", use a very soft through action which begs the question, how do you land a big fish on a soft rod?

Anglers use Wands all the time on commercial snake lakes and other very short range waters. Although feeder fishing is not a method for catching specimen fish, Carp in the low doubles are caught and successfully landed all the time. The difference is a decent fish cannot be bullied on light tackle, but with correctly balanced tackle, a hard fighting fish has to be successfully played out and brought to the net.

Rough guide to rod choice

The rough rod guide is just that, a rough guide. The casting distances may seem pessimistic, but in a strong wind these might be the best to expect. On a calm day though, it may be possible to cast a 30g feeder as much as 60m. Please bear in mind a feeder can weigh twice as much as the marked weight when full.

Always consult the manufacturer's specifications to confirm a rod is suited to your requirements before purchase.

Rod	Casting weight	Casting Distance	Tips in ounces	Reel size	Main line	Use
9ft	15g - 25g	25m - 30m	0.75, 1, 1.5	3000	2lb - 3lb	Silvers, small Carp and winter F1
9ft	25g - 35g	25m - 30m	0.75, 1, 1.5	4000	4lb - 6lb	Silvers, small Carp and winter F1
10ft	35g - 50g	30m - 40m	0.75, 1, 1.5, 2	4000	4lb - 8lb	Silverfish, Bream, F1s and small Carp
11ft	40g - 60g	40m - 50m	1, 1.5, 2	4000	4lb - 8lb or Braid	Silverfish, Bream, F1s and small to medium Carp
12ft	60g - 100g	60m plus	1, 1.5, 2, 3	5000	4lb - 10lb or Braid	Medium to long range 60m plus large stillwaters and rivers
13ft	100g - 150g	80m plus	2, 3, 4	5000 - 6000 Wide spool	Braid	Long range 80m plus ideal for large stillwaters and powerful rivers

Reels for feeder fishing

Fixed spool reels are the first best option. Sizes of 3000, 4000 and 5000 will cover all feeder fishing situations. In the guide to rod choice, I have recommended reels for the different rods. Beyond size, other reel specifications should be considered.

Most modern reels use a carbon fibre drag system to allow the smooth release of line when playing a good fish. Many manufacturers specify a maximum pulling force at which the drag on the reel will slip to let line out. Maximum drag ratings of 15lb to 25lb are common for the sizes of reels we are interested in. These values are way more than needed, but using a reel with a smooth drag is of greater importance.

Front or rear drag adjuster? My personal preference is for front drag. I like to play a fish with one hand on the spool to help control the release of line if a fish runs hard. I don't want to have to move my hand, or look down at the reel to make adjustments in the middle of playing a fish.

The more ball bearings a reel has, the smoother it operates. The number of bearings is expressed by two numbers, 4+1 or 9+1 for example. The first value is the number of bearings used in the mechanism of the reel. The +1 part refers to a roller bearing which also forms part of the infinite anti reverse mechanism. As a rule of thumb, the more ball bearings a reel has, the better the quality and more expensive.

Virtually every fixed spool reel made these days has infinite anti reverse, which simply means the anti reverse engages instantly in any position. With anti reverse switched on, the reel cannot be wound backwards to let line out. If a fish runs hard, the drag will slip letting line out as opposed to the angler back winding. Most fixed spool reels have a switch to engage or disengage the anti reverse, but there are some that don't, they only wind in. The option to backwind, even if it's just to let a little line out to cast or for a little slack to bring a feeder to the bait tub, is desirable.

Fishing reel gear ratio

Gear ratios describe the number of rotations of the rotor arm for each turn of the handle. Low ratios are better for reeling in end tackle that offers some resistance. High ratios are good for quick retrieval.

Common gear ratios between 4.3:1 to 4.8:1 provide an overall good line retrieval rate. High-speed ratios of 5.0:1 to 5.5:1 provide a quick retrieval rate for distance feeder fishing.

The amount of line retrieved depends on the gear ratio, but also the diameter of the spool. Some manufacturers state the line retrieval rate for each reel, which is perhaps a better guide to how fast the line is retrieved.

70cm or less - Slow line retrieve
80 to 90cm - Medium line retrieve
100cm plus - Fast line retrieval.

Wide spool reels

When casting to extreme range or casting into the wind, a wide spool reel can help in hitting the spot. The wider spool allows the main line to spill off easily improving casting distance. There are a handful of specialist wide spool feeder reels available usually in the larger sizes. Paired with powerful rods of 13ft or longer, casting distances of perhaps 100m can be achieved.

There is a limit as to how far a feeder can be cast. Although there are some weight forward (rocket) feeders designed to improve casting distance, having the skill, accuracy and power to cast one 100m or more time after time is a whole different matter.

Fishing reel main lines

There are only two types of line used in feeder fishing, nylon and braid. The two commonly used nylons are traditional monofilament and the heavier feeder monofilament. These two mono lines have different properties. Traditional mono has a neutral buoyancy, which means it can take longer to sink which is more of a problem at long range. One advantage of traditional mono is it has an amount of elasticity. This slight stretchiness is useful when hooking and playing fish at close range. For example, hooking a 15lb Carp on a snake lake at less than 20m. The stretch in traditional mono acts as an added buffer and helps to reduce hook pulls.

Feeder mono is a sinking line that has less stretch than traditional mono. As a sinking line, feeder mono is most useful when fishing at mid range and beyond. It is always desirable to use a main line that readily sinks down below any surface drift when fishing at distance. Feeder mono tends to be stiffer and have a higher memory, causing it to kink and twist more readily than traditional mono, so expect to replace it more often.

It would be unusual to use nylon much beyond 40m. The stretch in some nylon lines becomes unmanageable leading to poor bite indication and a lack of control playing fish further out. Braided lines have no stretch at all, allowing more direct contact with the fish solving both problems. Braided lines also have a much smaller diameter than nylon. The low diameter offers less resistance to the rod rings when casting, permitting greater distance. Braid cuts through the surface tension and sinks quickly and is less susceptible to undertow.

Although a braided line's lack of give improves in some aspects, it can be a problem on the cast and playing a fish under the rod tip at the net. At these times, a little give (stretchiness) is useful in reducing hook pulls, crack off's and perhaps your finger when casting.

Instead of using braid right through, a few metres of nylon is added above the end tackle. This "shock leader" acts as a buffer to soften the connection from rod to end tackle, an important addition which I will put in context later.

Line strengths and diameters

One advantage with feeder fishing over other methods, is that the main line lays on the bottom, no matter which type of feeder is attached to the end. Concerns over fish being spooked by the main line, although not removed, are much reduced. Using an inconspicuous hook link is of more importance, leaving the choice of main line purely a practical matter.

I believe most, if not all, feeder fishing can be done with just three main lines as follows.

Line	Type	Use
6lb - 0.22mm	Monofilament or sinking feeder mono	Winter fishing, micro feeders, small Carp, skimmers and silvers.
8lb - 0.25mm	Monofilament or sinking feeder mono	Summer, method feeder, Carp, Tench, Bream up to 40m
12lb - 0.10mm	Sinking feeder braid	Large waters, rivers, long distance, heavy feeders of all types.

In most situations these three main lines will suffice, but there will be some venues that require something different. Some commercials have waters boasting good stocks of double figure Carp. If you are lucky enough to fish a place like this, consider using a 12lb line of either type to be on the safe side. Other waters may occupy the opposite end of the scale and be stocked with small fish, in which case main lines down to 3lb breaking strain make sense. Local knowledge may often override common practises, it's up to the angler to decide best practise on any given water.

Balanced tackle

In other disciplines of angling, balancing the correct rod, size of reel and strength of line to the method of fishing is relatively simple. Standard kit for specimen Carp for example, might be a 12ft, 2½lb test curve rod, a 10000 size reel loaded with 12lb line. At the other end of the scale, a float fishing setup could be a 12ft, 1lb test curve rod, a 3000 size reel with 3lb line. The Carp example uses a stiff rod, big reel, strong line designed for big, hard fighting fish. In the second, a very light delicate setup is more suited to outwit the naturally cautious silvers. The balance between rod, reel and strength of line in both these setups is easy to understand. Feeder fishing though breaks the rules, it is quite possible to have 12lb braid on a heavy rod and reel casting 60m to catch 2lb Bream.

Weight of the feeder for casting distance or the flow of a river is the key factor in deciding which equipment to use. A comparison might be fly fishing where the line weight matches the rod. In feeder fishing the equipment needs to suit the weight needed to reach the spot or overcome conditions. This raises the question, how to play and land fish on tackle that is not suited to their size? The solution rests on the skill of the angler, the action of the rod, a correctly set reel drag and of course balanced tackle.

Rod rests and setup on the bank

There are three fundamental types of rod rest, smooth feeder, rippled feeder and quiver tip. At first glance they all do the same thing, hold the rod, but they are designed with different purposes in mind.

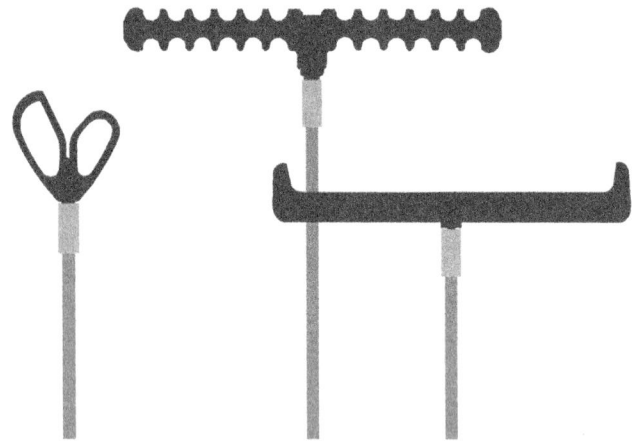

Fig 1: Three types of rod rest.

Quiver tip rod rests are primarily designed for river use. They are made to firmly hold a rod steady against the flow of a river pulling against the rod tip. The notches are shaped to hold the rod firmly yet allow an unhindered strike.

Rippled feeder rests hold a rod securely without trapping the line. I regard these as a general purpose rod rest which can be used in most situations.

Smooth feeder arms allow fine adjustment to the rod's position to get the tip just right. Or the rod can be moved along the rest a few inches to twitch the hookbait to draw attention resulting in a bite.

Backrest

There are two types of backrest, gripping and non-gripping. A non-gripping back rest is just a simple 'U' or 'V' shaped bankstick attachment to rest the rod butt in. A gripping back rest holds, grips, the butt of the rod. These are useful when full blooded takes are expected which threaten to pull the rod in. Carp especially are known for unexpectedly tearing off across the lake, which they do whenever you glance away or pick up your flask.

A backrest to hold the butt of the rod may not be necessary on those red letter days when the fish are coming thick and fast. On slower days there is time to put the rod down between fish to save holding the rod in your lap.

Rod position

Rod rests should be arranged to hold the rod tip close to the water surface. An angle of 45° to the swim (patch of water targeted) will be more than enough to register all bites. Whether the rod is arranged to one side or at an angle in front is down to your preferred way to strike.

On a fast or powerful river, it may be necessary to have the rod pointing skyward to hold as much line as possible out of the flow. This does mean looking up at the rod tip the whole session, but if that's what it takes...

Basic skills

Casting a feeder

In the early days of feeder fishing, the method was often associated with long distance fishing. There was an element of truth in this as fishing at less than 25yds was the realm of the float. Over the years feeder fishing has developed into a method in it's own right, not just something done when fishing beyond the range of a float. Today no one bats an eyelid at an angler casting a feeder very short distances. The only matter of importance is being able to put the feeder down more or less in the same spot each time. It is common practice to select a fixed object on the far bank as a marker to cast towards. Landing on that line time after time requires a great deal of practice. Any flaws in casting technique are exaggerated at greater distances, direction being the most likely to suffer.

Setup to cast

Aiming at the fixed marker on the far bank begins with stance. Align your body exactly facing the target. Sitting or standing, your feet should be parallel and pointing at the target. Resist the temptation to place one foot in front of the other, as this stance will cause the body, arms and shoulders to point to one side of the line.

Although at first it may feel unnatural to directly face the far bank marker, it has proven to be the best starting position as it really enhances the feeling of casting at the marker.

Line drop

The amount of line let out for the cast has a strong influence on trajectory. A short amount of line hanging from the rod tip will act to produce a low straight cast over the water. Too much line out will cause a high trajectory cast reducing overall distance, all the casting effort ends up going into height. The line drop from the tip of the rod should be somewhere in between, usually on or less than halfway down the rod. The line drop will be different from rod to rod, but start at a third of the length of the rod and adjust until it feels right and casts correctly.

Prepare to cast

Hold the rod in your dominant hand with the reel foot between your fingers. It is not important which fingers, so long as the lip of the spool can be reached with the tip of your index finger. Give the main line above the reel a couple of pulls to make sure the line is moving freely in the rings and that it has not become wrapped around the tip. Hook the main line behind your index finger and open the bail arm. Hold the end of the butt in your free hand.

Swing and cast

With the rod in front of your body and pointing at the target, gently swing the feeder out towards the far bank marker. As the feeder reaches the top of it's swing, bring the rod back behind you. Cause the feeder to swing over your head, keeping it on the line to the far bank marker.

As the feeder swings out behind, it will reach a point where it has swung back as far as it can and you will feel the weight of the feeder pulling on the rod. At this point the rod is pulled and curved down by the weight of the feeder. The rod is now loaded and straining to let rip.

Cast the rod forward by pushing with your dominant hand while using your butt hand as the pivot. Releasing the line from under your index finger at about mid cast. The loading in the rod and the effort of the angler will fling the feeder out into the lake. The cast should finish with the rod butt in the centre of your body and the shaft in line with the far bank marker.

Follow the feeder in the air with the tip of the rod allowing the line to spill from the reel. As the feeder approaches the surface, feather the line by lightly pressing your index finger against the spool to control the release of line. The whole cast from start to finish should be made as one smooth movement from the first swing out to following the feeder down.

Accuracy of direction

The cast described, does everything to land the feeder along the desired line, but the greater the distance cast, the greater the chance of casting off line. While aligning your body to face the far bank marker, swing the feeder out, then back over your head along the same line. Be conscious of keeping everything moving on the line and aiming at the far bank marker.

In ideal conditions, just keeping everything on target is enough, but if the wind gets up it will push the feeder off line. Casting slightly to one side of the line against the wind to compensate is the only answer.

Although casting overhead is the most accurate way, there will be times when casting from one side is necessary. In a side wind, feeder rigs that have a long hook link hanging down can catch on the rod. Practice casting in the same way, but instead of swinging the feeder back over your head. Swing the feeder back and behind to one side of your body allowing the wind to blow a long hook link away from the rod.

Setting casting distance

Casting distance can be set very accurately with the aid of the reels line clip. Every fixed spool reel made for feeder fishing will have a line clip on the skirt of the spool, most of which look like a small button.

There are two common ways to decide casting distance. The first is to arbitrarily pick a distance. I notice though, many anglers like to use 50m as a starting distance on a large water, with a backup of 30m. These are such common lines, I believe fish come to expect to find food along the 50m and 30m lines.

To set the line clip at whatever preselected distance desired, two bank sticks are first pushed into the bank 3m apart. The end of the line is placed on or around one stick. Using the tip of the rod, line is taken from one stick to the next counting each three metre of line taken. For 30m, ten passes from one stick to the other and for 50m, 16 and two third passes. Once measured the distance is fixed by passing the line behind the line clip. With the line clipped, each cast will stop at the same distance.

There will of course be fisheries where the 50m line is not suitable because of rocks, deep silt or it's an area the fish simply don't like. Which brings us to the second option, selecting a spot to cast to followed by measuring the distance. Local knowledge, experience or watercraft are used to decide where exactly to drop the feeder.

Cast towards your chosen spot in the lake. Control the feeder down and lift the rod upright as the feeder approaches the water. As the feeder lands, trap the line against the lip of the spool with your finger. Find the line clip on the spool skirt and pass the line under it. Personally I prefer to pass the line only once around the back of the clip. Others prefer to wrap from the front and then around behind the clip making one complete turn, that's up to you.

On the next cast as the feeder approaches the surface, hold the rod vertically above your head. As the escaping line reaches the line clip, it will abruptly stop, halting the feeder mid flight over the desired spot. Allow the rod to absorb the shock of this sudden stop.

After fine adjustments over several casts, the distance can be measured by the number of turns around the measuring sticks and noted for future reference. An alternative way to measure the distance is to count the number of turns on the reel needed to bring the rig back. This second method is not as useful as measuring sticks, because different reels retrieve at different rates.

Casting to the line clip and landing the feeder

A third element in casting a feeder, is keeping the feed on or in the feeder as it hits the surface of the water. Feeder design and consistency of the feed used within it play a part, but causing the feeder to land correctly helps enormously. Every cast should be made in such a way as to cause the feeder to drop into the water as opposed to crashing in. An uncontrolled cast will allow the feeder to enter the water at an angle and at great speed washing all the feed from it.

On every cast, the feeder needs to drop into the water as lightly as possible, falling almost vertically. Two variables need to change for a soft landing, the speed of the feeder and the angle of descent. A high trajectory could reduce both, but at the cost of distance. Using less force in the cast might help, but again at the cost of distance. Changing the force behind the cast or the path it follows does not hold the answer. Instead, controlling the last few yards of flight of the feeder is where the solution lies.

On those occasions when the line clip is employed, it can double up as a means to control how a feeder lands. The feeder can be made to land as gently as possible, by purposefully aiming to cast just beyond the distance set, then using it to slow the feeder in the last few feet of flight. To ensure the feed does not fly off the feeder as it slows. Or that the feed isn't washed off by the rebound of the rod pulling it back through the water on splashdown. The rod is used to control precisely how the feeder decelerates.

The object is to slow the feeder almost to a standstill, but without causing any retrograde motion when the rod rebounds from the shock of halting the feeder.

As mentioned above, cast the feeder and prepare to stop it at the correct distance by holding the rod vertically overhead. The line clip will stop the line at the correct distance and the rod will absorb the initial shock. It is at this point when the rod overcomes the forward motion of the feeder, that it will spring back pulling the feeder towards you. To prevent the unwanted bounce back of the feeder, the angler must allow the rod to move forwards lessening or better still preventing any pull back on the feeder. To achieve this, the rod cannot be held rigid after initially absorbing the feeder's forward movement. Instead the rod is moved forward, allowing it to straighten without pulling the feeder back. I like to imagine the feeder stopping in mid-air and in that instant moving the rod tip forward taking all the spring out of the rod. From that point the feeder will plop as gently as possible into the water. The knack is holding the rod firmly enough to stop the feeder, but then relaxing enough to allow the rod to bounce forwards without pulling the feeder back. The acid test is how the feeder lands. If the feeder plops cleanly into the water on the right spot consider it a good cast. If the feeder lands with any kind of splash, well, better luck on the next cast.

Casting unclipped and landing the feeder

In the cold temperatures of winter, fish shoal together in the warmest areas of the lake. The problem for the angler is locating these shoals to stand any chance of catching.

Instead of casting to the same old line used in the summer, an angler will have to find the shoals by literally casting about. The usual practice is to cast to the most likely looking spot and watch for any signs of fish. If after a time there are no signs of life, then reel in and cast elsewhere. A line clip is of little use until the fish are located, only then is it worth using.

Landing a feeder gently without the aid of the line clip is only a matter of slowing it's flight by feathering it down hard. Don't be tempted to hook your finger behind the line, especially braid, just press harder against the lip of the spool to slow the release of line.

Another concern voiced with "clipping up" is the thought of a big fish taking line up to the line clip and causing the line to break. My solution has always been to only pass the line behind the clip and not around it. If then I hook a powerful fish, I can quickly reach in and unclip the line before it's broken. Needless to say, the window of opportunity to unclip mid-fight is very short, but by no means impossible.

The feeder has landed

Once the feeder has sunk to the bottom, place the rod in the rod rests and carefully tighten down to the feeder until a slight bend is pulled into the rod tip. At no point should the feeder be allowed to move. If the feeder is disturbed, it could easily pull under the mud or debris on the bottom, turn over.

Plumbing the depth with a bomb

Gathering information about where you are fishing is always a prerequisite to catching. Knowing the water depth and physical features of the lake or river bed are basic essentials. Water depth can be easily measured by timing how long it takes for a square bomb to sink to the bottom.

Cast out and feather the line down keeping in contact with the bomb right to the surface. As the bomb hits, hold the rod steady keeping a bend in the tip against the sinking bomb. Begin counting or timing while holding the rod still. The rod tip will spring straight when the bomb lands on the bottom.

To get a full picture of the contours and depths, use a systematic approach starting to one side at close range. Cast out 20m and time the bombs descent. Cast out to 30m, 40m and so on, timing the drop on each cast. Repeat the process in front and to the right. After a few casts the shape of the bottom can be mapped. Knowing the shape of the bottom will be a great help in deciding where to fish.

Most anglers use a 30 or 40 gram square bomb, although it doesn't matter too much which weight of bomb is used. A 30g bomb will sink about 20 feet in 8 seconds or roughly 1m/sec. I recommend using the same bomb at every venue to provide continuity.

Counting how long it takes for a bomb to sink may not be very accurate, but in feeder fishing, an overview of the depth and contours of the bottom is enough. The bomb can also be used to get an idea of what the bottom is like.

Drag the bomb along the bottom with the rod and feel how the bomb moves. If the bomb moves in jumps and jerks, the bottom is covered in snags, debris or rocks. It could also be soft silt, but the bomb will feel as if it is getting stuck then releasing over and over. A bomb dragged across rocks will not feel soft in it's movements, it will jump and jerk in a sharper, harder way.

All forms of feeder fishing perform best on a smooth firm bottom. Time spent measuring the depth and locating a clear smooth area is time well spent. Braided main lines transmit how the bottom feels far better than mono, as the stretchiness of mono tends to deaden the vibrations up the line. Use braid to feel the bottom even if you then have to change to mono to fish.

The depth of water in a river, lake or reservoir will change with the seasons or tide. So knowing the exact depth is less important than knowing the contours and the makeup of the bottom. Allowances can be made for changes in depth, but casting to an unsuitable bottom will greatly reduce your chance of catching.

Flatbed feeders

Flatbed feeders consist of a flat weight with a bait compartment on top. The bait compartment can be a bowl or frame which is used to carry free offerings together with the hookbait out to the fish.

The flat weight on the bottom ensures the feeder always lands the right way up, with the food uppermost. A short baited hook link is attached and buried within the feed. When a fish sucks feed off of the feeder, the hookbait is sucked up at the same time.

Then, as the fish lifts it's head or moves away in any direction, the short hook link tightens against the feeder. The weight of the feeder tethered to the hook link will cause the hook to prick the fish inside it's mouth. The fish will Immediately realise it has been hooked and bolt.

Inline flatbed feeders

There are many variations in design, size and weight of flatbed feeders, but the general principle of using the weight of the feeder to hook the fish stands for all of them.

There are two common ways to attach a flatbed feeder to the main line, either directly or inline. Any ledger rig tied directly to the line is known as a fixed rig. Fixed rigs are very efficient at causing the fish to self hook, but because the weight is tied directly to the line, they are very unsafe for the fish. If for any reason the main line were to break, a fish could potentially become self hooked to the rig and feeder. A fish will not live long dragging a heavy weight around. It is for this reason that fixed rigs are not used by responsible anglers and are banned by fishery owners.

Please do not use fixed rigs.

An inline feeder is much safer because the main line is not directly attached to the feeder. The line is instead threaded through the feeder. If the main line should break, it will pull through leaving the feeder safely on the bottom. The fish will still have a hook in it's mouth, which it will shed in time, but more importantly the fish can continue to behave and feed normally.

There is one other system which was designed to make fixed rigs safer and reduce hook pulls. Elasticated feeders are fixed rigs with a short length of strong elastic built into the feeder. The theory goes that the main line is tied to the end of the elastic, which helps to absorb the jerks and lunges of a hooked fish. Supporters of elasticated feeders also claim the buffering action of the elastic reduces hook pulls, especially when the fish is close in under the rod tip while netting. In my opinion, the line will not break or the hook pull, if the angler is using a correctly set drag and balanced tackle. I believe netting the fish is safe when using the correct tackle and after playing the fish out. Many fishery owners have banned elasticated feeders, so please check the fishery rules first.

Setting up an inline feeder

Thread the main line through the feeder, and tie the swivel provided to the end. Use either a Uni knot or Palomar knot which are both strong and reliable knots. Slide the feeder down the line and pull the swivel into the rubber bush in the front of the feeder. Attach the hook link by passing the loop through the swivel eye, then pass the hook through the loop and pull down tight.

The swivel used in creating the rig should be a snug fit in the front of the feeder. This may appear to make an outlawed fixed rig, but it does not. If the main line was to break, the fish would only be tethered to the feeder for a short time before the swivel pulled free of the feeder. Although the swivel should be a snug fit, it should still pull free when needed.

A semi fixed rig such as this enhances self hooking, yet remains safe and is approved by most fisheries.

An alternative to a swivel which has gained popularity recently, is the quick change connector or quick change bead. The main line is tied to the connector by trapping it within a figure-of-eight loop knot.

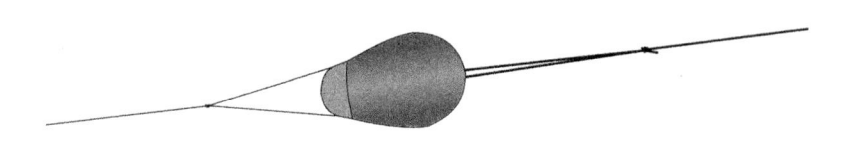

Fig 2: Quick change connector.

Connector beads sit in front of the feeder allowing the feeder to be completely free running, which is the safest rig arrangement and permitted by the majority of fisheries. Despite the loss of the bolt effect, the rig still works well, mainly because of the extreme sharpness of modern hooks, although this does mean replacing the hook more frequently.

Small light micro feeders often used in winter use a custom design of quick change connector. It is designed to fit snugly into the front of the feeder making a semi fixed rig. These have proven to be more successful with these light weight feeders than a free running rig.

Hook links

The next part of the rig is the hook link. The hook link is a short piece of line connecting the hook to the main line through the swivel or quick connector. At the front end is of course the hook, with a figure-of-eight loop connection at the other end.

Hook links can be tied from monofilament or fluorocarbon. Some recommend the use of braid because of it's suppleness, but it's thin diameter can act like a cheese wire on the fish's mouth, so please don't use braid.

There are conflicting opinions as to the best length of a hook link, but all agree the most practical length is 4 inches measured from the hook bend. At times when the fish are lethargic, in the cold perhaps, a shorter 2 or 3 inch length can be useful. Personally I stick to 4 inches all year round, but I may use a lighter line in the cold.

Hooks for flatbed feeders

To enhance the self-hooking properties of flatbed feeder rigs, the hook needs to be exposed. The point must be sharp and designed to stand the best chance of pricking the fish's mouth. Over the years I have found two patterns of hook in which I place my faith. The first is a wide gape, short shanked hook. The gape is the opening between the shank and the point. A wide opening in combination with a short shank, increases the chance of the hook point catching as the hook link tightens to the feeder.

The second pattern of hook is a circle hook. Circle hooks were originally used by sea anglers for their "hook and hold" properties. The unique shape of the bend in these hooks means the fish find them very difficult to shed once hooked. The only drawback with circle hooks is the narrow gape. I believe circle hooks of less than size 10 have such a narrow gape, that it makes them less likely to catch at the critical moment. I recommend the short shank wide gape patterns for hooks smaller than a size 10. Use bigger baits for bigger fish, with circle hooks of size 10 and larger.

Another important element of hook design in the context of flatbed feeders, is how the hook is presented on the line. A short hook link tied from what is often quite stiff material, can cause a hook with an inline eye to sit at an angle. I appreciate specimen Carp anglers may recommend this arrangement, but for the smaller hooks used in flatbed feeder fishing I believe it is better for the hook shank to align with the line.

Circle hook

Wide gape hook with out turned eye

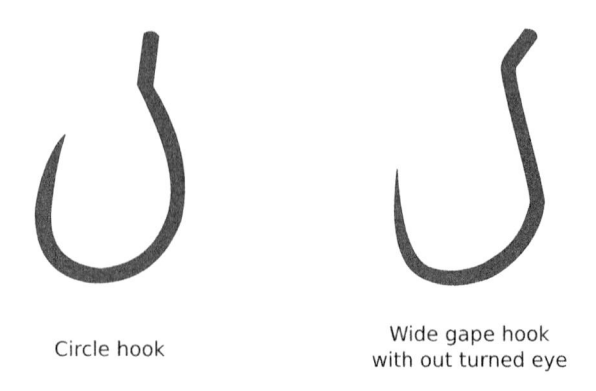

Fig 3: Circle and wide gape hooks.

Use hooks with an out turned eye, they align far better with the hook link line offering a better presentation. Bigger hooks, 8's and 6's perhaps, may be used in a straight eyed pattern, if the fish expected are big enough.

Tying a hook link

No matter which bait is used with a flatbed feeder, the hook point must be exposed to ensure it easily pricks the inside of the mouth. A number of clever devices and baits have been developed to present a bait while leaving the point exposed. All of these devices are designed to hold the bait just under the hook bend, in a way that is very close to being hooked directly. All the common bait holding devices are connected to the hook by a piece of line called a hair. The hair is made from one end of the knot used to tie the hook on.

Fig 4: Hook with hair.

Knotless knot - hair rig

The decision as to which bait holding device to employ, has to be made when tying the hook to the link line. This is because the first step is preparing what will be the hair in the finished knot and including the device you intend to use. Pellet band, quick stop and Bayonet are the three most popular and practical devices commonly used.

Pellet band

A pellet band is literally a tiny latex rubber band. The band is attached to the hair and wrapped around a piece of bait to hold it close to the hook. Ideal for hard pellets and dumbbell shaped baits. The band has to be included when tying the hook to the link line.

Fig 5: Pellet band rig.

To tie a flatbed feeder hook link to an eyed hook with a hair rigged pellet band, begin by threading a pellet band onto a length of line. Tie a small overhand loop with the band inside the loop. The loop only needs to be about the same length as the shank of the hook. Cut the tag end of the loop close to the knot to leave a tight, neat knot.

Thread the opposite end of the line through the back of the eye and pull the loop up to the hook. The optimum place for the bait band to sit is just below the bend in the hook, putting a pellet in the band can help in judging the best place.

While holding the hair in place against the shank, wrap the line around the shank, trapping the hair as you go, from the eye down the shank towards the bend. The first couple of turns should be above the knot of the loop, going to below the knot and over the loop as the wraps progress down the shank. Once the turns of line around the shank become parallel with the hook point, hold everything in place while threading the end of the line back through the hook eye from back to front. The link line should exit the eye on the side that faces the hook point, in other words, the inside. Pull the knot tight ensuring all the wraps around the shank are neat and tidy. The bait band should be able to move freely on the little bit of loop left exposed and hang just below the hook bend.

With the hook tied, it's just a matter of tying a loop on the other end to finish. A strong loop knot will be needed as it will take all the strain when playing a fish. The very best loop knot in my experience is the figure-of-eight loop knot, which I will attempt to describe.

To get every hook link exactly the same length, a jig with two pegs, (nails perhaps) set four inches apart will be of great help. Hook the hook behind one peg, bring the line up and around the second and back towards the first. Grasp both half together to form a loop. With your free hand, pull the line off of the second peg by sliding the line up and off.

Do not release the line by pulling it anywhere in between, as you will almost certainly change the length, just pull directly from the second peg. You should now have a loop of the correct length in the line ready to tie.

Double the loop over with your free hand and grasp it in between the same fingers holding the original loop. Put your freehand finger and thumb through the doubled loop and twist the loop 180°. Grasp the end of the original loop and pull it through the double loop. Whilst all the time holding the original line, manipulate the knot up the line to create a loop of 10 to 15mm, or big enough to pass the hook and band through. Moisten the knot with saliva before pulling tight. If the knot fell apart after the twist, try again but twist in the opposite direction, in effect you are wrapping around the original line going the wrong way won't work.

Figure of eight loop knot

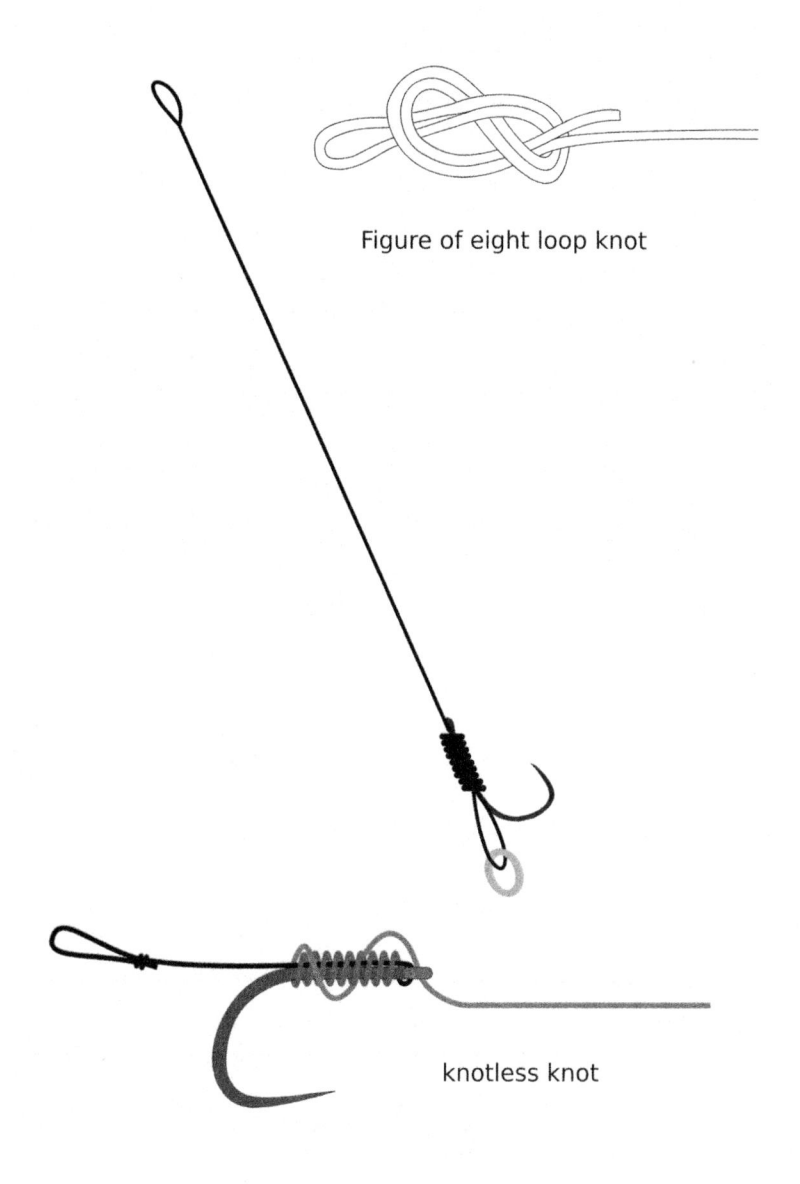

knotless knot

Fig 6: Completed hook and hair rig.

Cut off the tail end leaving a short tag. The knot itself takes up some of the line, although the two pegs on the jig are 4" apart, the whole hook link will be a tad shorter. Bear this in mind if storing in a hook link box, although monofilament should stretch the small amount needed to fit.

Quick stop

In the context of the flatbed feeder, a quick stop is used to hold softer baits on the hair. Baits like sweetcorn, mini boilies and soft pellets. The idea is to push the quick stop through the bait and turn the stop 90° to keep the bait on the hair. The blunt end of the stop is hollow to mount on a tool for pushing the stop through the bait. To mount firm or hard baits which might split or break apart, drill a hole through the bait first. Many of the bait manufacturers supply pre-drilled hard pellets to save you the job of drilling.

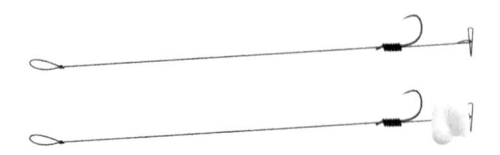

Fig 7: Hook with quick stop and bait.

The quick stop is tied within a small loop before tying to the hook with a knotless knot. Because a quick stop can be used with any size and shape of bait, it is useful to thread the bait onto the line to judge the correct distance from the hook, especially if using double corn, a large bait or a bait combination. Allow a gap of around 5 mm between the hook band and the bait.

Once the position of the hook has been decided, tie the hook with a knotless knot as previously described. The small loop in the end of the hair should remain well outside of the knot. This permits maximum flexibility in the hair allowing large, double or even triple baits to move out of the way of the hook point to increase the chance of hooking a fish.

Bait bayonet

A bayonet is a small metal spike commonly made of twisted wire which firmly grips a skewered bait of the correct firmness. Boilies, Wafters, hookers and various artificial baits work well with bayonets.

Begin the rig by tying a bayonet within a small overhand loop. Tie the hook on with a knotless knot ensuring the eye of the bayonet aligns with the bottom of the bend. Trap the small loop of line under the whippings and whip right down to opposite the point. The bayonet will then be restricted to a very small loop, but remain loose to allow the bait to behave naturally. To mount a bait, just push the bayonet into the bait right up to the eye.

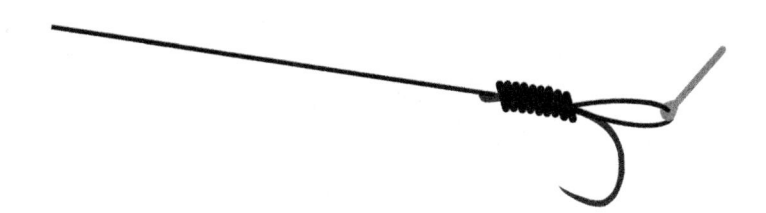

Fig 8: Hair rig with bayonet.

Baits to use with a flatbed feeder

When a fish discovers a loaded feeder on the lake bed, it sucks all the feed up along with the hookbait, then gets snagged on the hook as it lifts it's head or moves away. It is understandable to imagine the type of hookbait would make little difference as it's just part of the pile, yet it so very often does. Consistency, colour and size can all play a part in catching fish, so let's run through some of the most successful hookbaits.

Hookbaits

Hard pellets

Used straight from the bag, sinking coarse pellets are one of the easiest hookbaits to use with a flatbed feeder. No special preparation needed, simply use a pellet band to hold them in place by the hook. To get them in the pellet band, either pull the band on with your fingers or use a pellet banding tool. A pellet banding tool stretches the latex band open allowing a pellet to be slipped inside, the tool is then pulled away while holding the band in place.

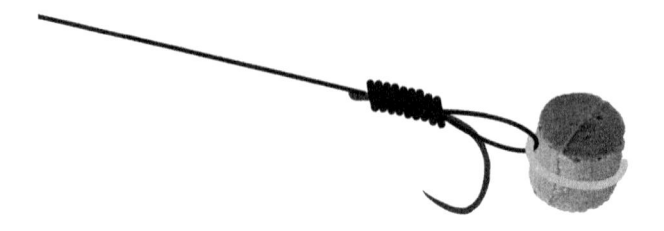

Fig 9: Banded pellet.

The best sizes of pellets to use are 6mm and 8mm hard pellets. As a rule of thumb, 8mm with a 12 or 14 hook are for the summer months when the fish, Carp in particular, are actively feeding. The smaller 6mm pellets on a 14 to 18 hook tend to be better in the colder weather from November to April or May when the fish are less interested.

Hookers (soft pellets)

As their name suggests, soft hooker pellets are made to be put directly on the hook in the traditional way. Although there is nothing to say you can't do this when flatbed feeder fishing, to do so would reduce the rig's effectiveness. Soft hooker pellets can be banded in the same way as hard pellets, or they can be secured with the quick stop or bayonet, depending on how firm they are.

Ignoring the range of colours and flavours for the moment, the quality that sets them apart from hard pellets is clearly their texture. There are times when their softer texture simply produces more bites, which is why I always carry a few 6mm, 8mm and 10mm with me.

Expanders

Expander pellets are rock hard out of the bag. Hydrate in water to change them into a very soft pellet which Carp absolutely love. Expanders are usually too soft to band, but they can be put directly on the hook with the right preparation.

The usual way to hydrate expander pellets is with a pellet pump. A handful of pellets are immersed in water inside the pump, which when pumped, forces the air out of the pellets causing them to quickly soak up the water.

To produce a slightly firmer pellet more suited for use on a flatbed feeder, it is better to soak them in cold water. One method is to put some pellets in a thermos flask with cold water and a couple of ice cubes and let them soak overnight. A second method is to drop enough pellets for a session into the corner of a plastic bag. Add just enough water to cover the pellets and tie a knot in the bag to tightly seal them in. Leave as little room as possible for the pellets to expand, then put the bag in a fridge overnight. Once ready, either method will produce a hydrated pellet firm enough to hook directly and use with a feeder.

Boilies

Boilies, as used by specimen Carp anglers, are a spherical bait with a soft centre and a firm outer layer. Mini boilies are a good choice for flatbed feeders and come in a vast range of flavours and colours. Some contain enhancers and attractants, others have strong spicy or sweet flavours. Spherical boilies can be bayoneted and dumbbells can be banded or bayoneted. Boilies are heavier than water and will sink and stay on the feeder or bottom.

Wafters

Wafters are semi buoyant boilies designed to counterbalance the weight of the hook. The idea is that a feeding fish will suck the Wafter up very easily along with the hook. Like boilies, Wafters come in a range of flavours and colours, but without doubt the bright and or fluorescent colours are the most popular. An ideal presentation is for the hook to be laying flat with the

Wafter hovering over it. This makes the bait both easy to find and sucked up by the fish.

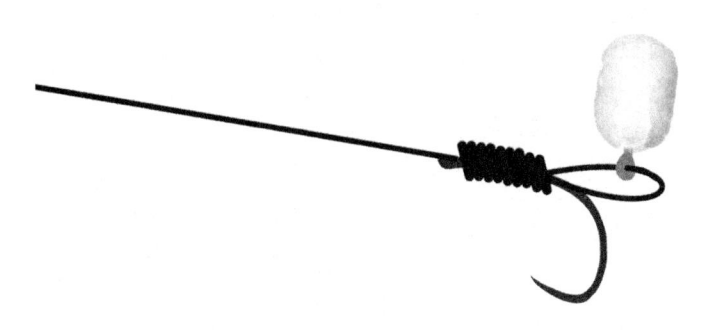

Fig 10: Bayonetted Wafter.

Pop-ups

Pop-ups are the most buoyant of all the boilie type baits, so much so that they will lift the hook and hook link off the feeder. They are designed to pop up above the bottom to make them very visible to the fish, especially in clear water. Once again they come in a vast range of colours and flavours, but their main advantage is their visibility. A good presentation is to have a pop-up hovering over the feeder and bait.

Boosters, liquids and sprays

A large selection of boosters, liquids and sprays can be used to coat any of the hookbaits to make them more appealing. Some anglers go as far as to coat the feeder once it is loaded for even more attraction.

Feed baits

To fulfil it's purpose to both attract and hook fish, a flatbed feeder needs to carry both feed as well as a hookbait. There are two primary types of feed bait, pellets and groundbait. Flatbed feeders were originally developed by match anglers for catching Carp on commercial fisheries. The vast majority of Carp caught in commercials are farmed fish, which were raised and grown on with fish pellets. So it's no big surprise that fishing with pellets on a commercial is preferred as the fish already have a taste for them. Wild fish in natural waters may not have seen a pellet before, but because pellets were developed to provide fish with everything nutritionally they need, wild fish quickly cotton on.

Groundbait is bait powder used mainly to attract fish without necessarily feeding them. Groundbaits can often be nothing more than ground down pellets or bread crumbs. Alternatively, groundbaits can be complicated mixes of different food stuffs and flavourings, it all depends on what the groundbait is being used for.

In flatbed feeder fishing, groundbait is used to put out a "food here" signal as a cloud of colour and flavours in the water and on the lake bed. It can also double up as a binder to hold pellets or other feed particles together on the feeder during the cast and down to the bottom. Although pellets are the most popular feed to use, groundbait allows the use of feeds that don't naturally stay on a feeder, like hemp for example.

Preparing pellets

Hard pellets are bone dry out of the bag and are never going to stay on a feeder without some preparation. To get the pellets to stick together they need to be dampened. Covering them with lake water is the easiest way either with a quick dip or by soaking.

Dampening pellets

Put a pint of pellets in a bait tub. Cover them in water. Allow them to soak for roughly one minute per millimetre in size. Soak 2mm pellets for two minutes, 3mm pellets for three minutes and so on. Drain them off and let them stand for 20 minutes. Water soluble pellet dyes, flavourings or binding agents can be added to the water, or sprinkled on the finished pellets if in powder form.

Soaking time will differ from one type of pellet to another. Low oil pellets take on water more quickly than an oily brand. Generally the darker coloured pellets have more oil. If the pellets get too wet they may disintegrate into a mush which is no use on a feeder. Ensure the pellets are tacky enough to stick together, yet separate cleanly on the lake bed. The only other point I would make is not to prepare too many at a time, as they will dry out during the day and lose their stickiness.

Groundbait

In the context of the flatbed feeder, groundbait is most commonly used as a binding agent. It is used to help hold together dampened pellets or particles of food that are not normally tacky. Any of the method mix, margin mix or river mix groundbaits can serve to bind particles on a flatbed feeder. Groundbaits made from crushed pellets also work well.

All of these groundbaits are quite tacky and designed to attract bottom feeding fish. They tend to be passive, in other words inert until disturbed. Although they break down over a few minutes releasing the feed, they do not actively throw particles up into the water column. Some taste or odour may emanate to attract the fish, but on the whole these groundbaits stay on the lake bed until stirred up by feeding fish.

Fishmeal and sweet fishmeal blends are very effective at attracting Bream and Carp. Cereal blends containing an active ingredient like Hemp would only be used when there is a clear reason to.

On cold days or in the winter when overfeeding the fish is a real possibility, loading a feeder with just groundbait can provide a means of attracting some fish. Once over the feeder, the fish find nothing substantial to eat other than the hookbait. When the weather is cold and the fish have little appetite, a groundbait only approach may be the only way to hook a few fish.

Mixing groundbait

To prepare groundbait properly takes a good half an hour, so make it your first job before tackling-up. Generally about half a bag (two pints) of groundbait will last a five hour session flatbed feeder fishing. Pour the dry groundbait into a round container, a bucket or a bowl. Add small amounts of water whilst vigorously mixing, stop when the groundbait feels damp. It is important not to add too much water. If the groundbait gets too wet it can become either sloppy or heavy and sticky, neither of which is any use on a flatbed feeder. To my mind, it is better to mix the groundbait on the dry side, you can always add more water. Remove any lumps by sieving the damp groundbait through a maggot riddle, then leave it to stand for at least twenty minutes.

Upon returning, squeeze a handful of the groundbait into a ball. If the mix is ready the ball should be easy to form, yet disintegrate when rubbed between the hands. If a ball cannot be formed add a small amount of water, riddle and let stand for a few more minutes.

Hybrid and Banjo feeders

Hybrid and Banjo feeders are simply a flat weight with a bowl on top to carry the feed and hookbait to the bottom.

The Hybrid has an aerodynamic teardrop shape, ideal for casting. Some are "weight forward", in other words they have more weight at the wide front end to improve long distance casting and accuracy. Whereas the Banjo is a round shape ideal for shorter casts of up to 30 metres. Banjos can also be useful when fishing on a slope, their round shape makes them less likely to flip over and roll down the slope.

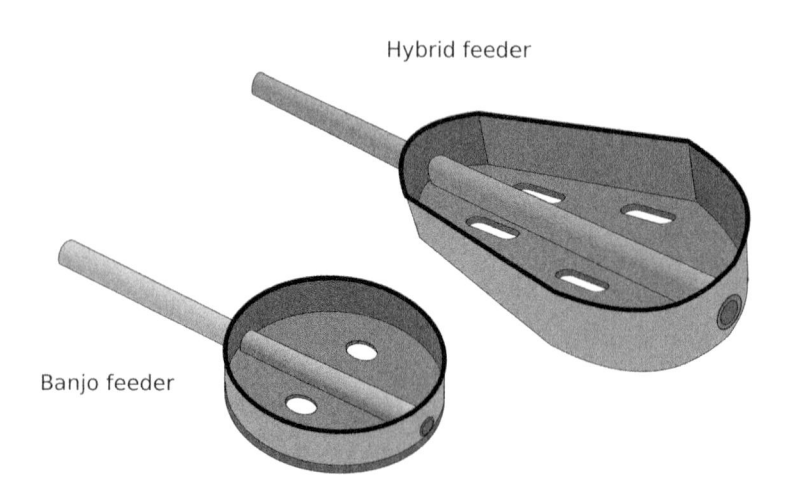

Fig 11: Hybrid and Banjo feeders.

Rigs for Hybrid and Banjo feeders

Most Hybrid/Banjo feeders consist of a tail rubber, the feeder body and a connector or swivel for attaching the hook link. To tie an inline rig, thread the tail rubber onto the mainline, followed by the feeder body. Use a Uni knot to tie a swivel to the end of the line. Attach the hook link, slide the feeder down the line and push the swivel into the rubber bush in the front of the body. Finally push the tail rubber over the end of the stem completing the rig, Fig.12.

Over the years improvements and variations have been developed, one trend is to use a plastic connector to join the main line to the hook link instead of a swivel. I have no doubt there will be other variations and redesigns yet to appear, but the basic principles will remain the same, setting a trap for the fish to get hooked on.

The trap consists of a bowl of free offerings with the hookbait hidden inside. The hope is that a fish will suck the free offerings along with the hookbait and get snagged on the hook as a consequence. To set the trap correctly, the feeder must arrive on the bottom with the feed and hookbait intact on the feeder. The hybrid feeder lends itself perfectly to this because the sides of the bowl offer some protection to the feed as the feeder sinks. As long as the feed placed within the feeder is tacky enough, it will remain in the feeder right to the bottom.

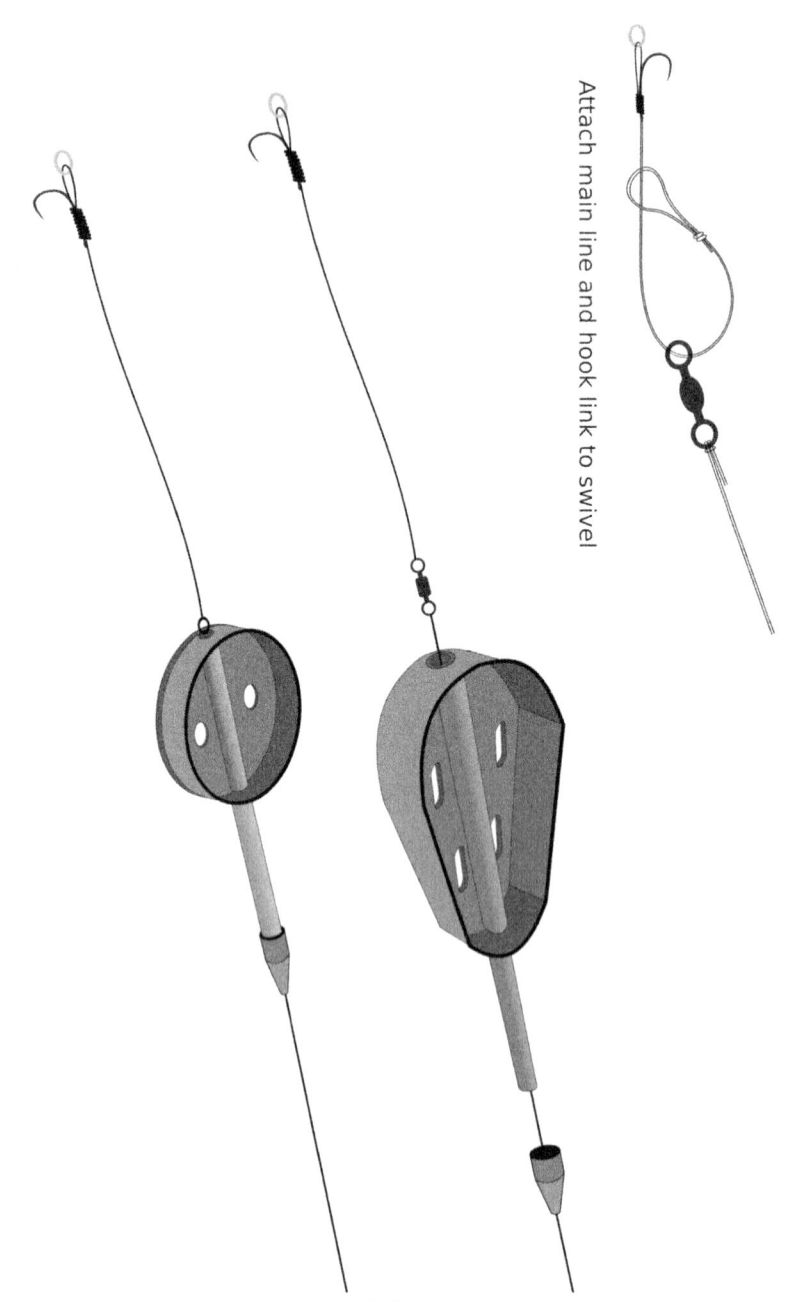

Fig 12: Hybrid and Banjo rigs.

Preparing pellets

As mentioned earlier, preparing hard pellets for use in a Hybrid feeder is just a matter of wetting them for a few minutes. As a rule of thumb, wet pellets for one minute per 1mm in size. Once wetted, it's important to immediately drain off any remaining water and allow them to stand for 20 minutes before use. The resulting bait should stick together if squeezed into a ball, but easily break apart back to individual pellets again.

Small or micro pellets of 2mm or maybe 3mm in size are best for the Hybrid and for that matter most other flatbed feeders. Larger pellets just don't stick together well without the addition of groundbait or some other binding agent.

Loading a Hybrid feeder

Loading the feeder is a two step process. First fill the bowl of the feeder level with dampened pellets and squeeze them down with your thumb. They can be squeezed as hard as you like and in fact I recommend they are given a good squeeze. Lay the hook and bait on top, ideally with the hook point uppermost. Pile a layer of pellets over the top to cover the hook and bait and squeeze them down to hold everything in place. The loaded feeder should be full with a bulge of pellets on top with the hook and bait hidden inside.

Cast the feeder out and control it's descent to ensure it "plops" into the water nicely. Try to keep the tip of the rod in contact with the feeder while it sinks to the bottom. The tip of the rod will spring back once the feeder has landed.

Plunge the rod tip below the water and very gently pull on the line to sink it from tip to feeder.

With all the line sunk, place the rod in it's rests. The rests should have been arranged to cause the rod tip to be just above the surface and at an angle to the line. Reel in a little to pull a slight bend into the tip ensuring good contact with the feeder.

On the lake bed, the feed will swell and expand out of the feeder with the topmost layer falling away to reveal the hookbait. The sides of the feeder will hold much of the feed together inside, presenting a mouthful of food with the hookbait on top, ideal for a fish to suck up in one go.

How the feed pellets are prepared has an influence on how effective the trap is. If the pellets are over wetted during preparation they will not take on more water to expand correctly on the lake bed. If they don't expand they will not push the hookbait to the top, worse still, they could stay in the feeder as one lump masking the hook. On the other hand if the pellets are too dry they may fly off on the cast or wash off as the feeder falls through the water. Correctly prepared pellets should stay on the feeder until it reaches the bottom. They should then expand enough to reveal the hookbait, but not so many that they spill out all around the feeder. This last point can result in fish picking up all the loose pellets around the feeder, rather than being left with only the pellets inside the feeder which contain the hook. To set the perfect Hybrid/ Banjo feeder trap, the feed has to be prepared just right.

I said previously, moisten the feed pellets by submerging them for one minute per 1mm, but this is only a guide. Different pellets have different ingredients which will absorb water at different rates. The only way to truly control how the pellets behave underwater is to run experiments with them. Dunk a few pellets at a time and vary how long they are left to soak to determine the optimum duration. I often do this at home, loading a feeder and dropping it in water to observe how the pellets react underwater. It all takes time and patience, but for best results it is the only way.

Loading a Banjo feeder

Unlike the Hybrid feeder, Banjo's are loaded with the aid of a mould. The mould is filled with pellets and the feeder is pressed onto the pellets, the opposite to how a Hybrid is loaded. The use of a mould has the advantage of creating a uniform, neatly presented trap every time the trap is set. Speaking personally, I find a mould particularly helpful when using small or micro feeders in the winter. Trying to fill a small feeder by hand is awkward enough, let alone in the cold.

Hookbait - part of the trap

In other forms of fishing, the hookbait is often a special morsel of food which is bigger, tastier or in some way stands out from the feed. Although in flatbed feeder fishing the same may be true, there is an additional property which needs to be understood. How the bait behaves when a fish comes to the feeder.

A feeder contains a mouthful of fish food along with the hookbait. The idea is that when a fish comes along, it sucks in all the bait off of the feeder including the hookbait. If the hookbait is the wrong size or can be sucked off the hair or spat out, then the fish escapes the trap.

Carp are usually the species in mind when using a Hybrid or Banjo feeder, but Carp are also a species which quickly learn how to avoid the dangers involved in eating convenient, neat piles of food laying on the bottom. Some will learn how to eat the feed pellets without picking up the hookbait. Others will eat all loose pellets around the feeder avoiding the hookbait. There are always going to be some daft fish that just never see the danger and get caught over and over, but with age, most Carp get wise. It follows then that no single bait will work in every situation on every Carp in the lake, it's a smart angler who carries a selection of hookbaits.

A banded hard pellet is, I believe, the most popular hookbait used with Hybrid/Banjo feeders. Pellets from 6mm to 10mm can be used with 8mm being by far the most popular. The popularity of 8mm sized hookbaits is not just down to conformity of anglers, 8mm baits are the ideal size and weight in most circumstances.

The optimum setup for these feeders is for the hookbait to be sitting in or on the feed contained within the bowl of the feeder. We don't want the hookbait to come out of the feeder and lay on the bottom to one side. If Carp are coming to the net hooked outside of the mouth, or the hook pulls within seconds, suspect the hookbait is not being presented correctly, which usually means the hook and bait had come out of the feeder.

The heavier hookbaits like hard pellets, micro boilies and dumbbells are generally a better option than Wafters for Hybrid/Banjo type flatbed feeders. It follows that small baits can also be too light, especially if used with a stiff hook link. Large hookbaits on the other hand can be difficult to use with small and medium sized feeders. They are best used with large feeders in waters that are stocked with a large head of big Carp.

To ensure the hookbait stays within the feeder for as long as possible, one option is to load the feeder with the hookbait in the bottom. Much advice on the internet and in the angling media suggest the hookbait should be at or near the top of the feed when loading. I feel this is too high and only encourages the hookbait to fall to the side more easily. To keep the hookbait within the sides of the feeder for longer, it is better to put the hookbait in the bottom of the feeder, or at least on a thin layer of pellets and piling the rest of the feed on top in the case of a Hybrid, or filling the mould and adding the hookbait last with a Banjo. Then, even if the top layers of feed wash away, the hookbait should stay inside the feeder.

Pellets and boilies do work well on these feeders, but they are not the only hookbait. There will be times when the fish get wise to hard or brightly coloured baits, on these occasions alternative softer baits can be better. For example, sweetcorn or dead maggots can transform a slow day.

There are no concerns in damaging a hard bait when loading the feeder, a soft bait on the other hand needs a slightly different approach. Begin as usual by squashing a layer of feed in the bottom of the feeder bowl.

Then place the soft hookbait on top, but instead of covering the bait with more feed, cover only the line and hook shank. Leave the hookbait exposed, only squeeze the top layer of pellets onto the line and hook shank. Soft hookbaits will need to be hooked either direct on the hook or with a quick stop. For example, hook maggots directly either singularly or in a bunch of two, three or more. I find dead red maggots to be the best. Sweetcorn, meat and other soft baits can be secured with a quick stop.

Fishing the Hybrid

The first consideration is always where to set your trap. It does not matter a jot how good your bait, rigs and tackle are if there are no fish where you have cast it. Factors such as the weather, makeup and geography of the lake bed, as well as fish behaviour all have to be taken into account.

It can be very difficult to "find the fish" on any particular day, especially if all the best pegs (marked sections of bank) are already taken when you arrive. If you are new to fishing, standing on the bank of a lake you have never fished can be daunting, but there are some things that are true whether you are a newbie or an expert.

Every lake is different, but in my view there are three fundamental types of fishery, natural waters, club waters and commercial waters. Clearly there are differences in size and depth, but success in Carp fishing with a flatbed feeder does depend on how many fish are in the lake. Commercially run fisheries tend to have a good stock of fish to ensure a high number of satisfied customers.

At the other end of the scale are the natural waters which tend to have far fewer Carp and a great many native species. Flatbed feeders like the Hybrid were originally designed by match anglers to rack up big weights at competitions held on commercial waters. Although the principle of a flatbed feeder works just as well on natural waters, the fact that there are not as many Carp usually means fewer fish on the bank. Fisheries run by private clubs can be regarded as a halfway house with mixed waters containing a respectable number of Carp along with other bottom feeders like Bream and Tench.

To get the most out of using a Hybrid or Banjo feeder the type of water must be taken into consideration. Waters with low stocks will require more planning, dedication and local knowledge to land a reasonable net of fish. Commercially run waters on the other hand offer the best chance for success.

One fish at a time

By design, the sides of a Hybrid/Banjo feeder keeps most of the feed in the bowl, not only during the cast, but also on the way to the bottom. A little feed may escape, but most of it should stay in the feeder along with the hookbait waiting for a fish.

As traps go the Hybrid is quite efficient, but it can only target one fish at a time. What I mean by that is a fish has to stumble across the feeder before there is any possibility of catching it. A Hybrid feeder on it's own offers one mouthful of food in a tight bundle in what could be acres of lake bed.

On the right day, on the right water, in the right place a Hybrid/Banjo feeder can be unbeatable, but as with all angling techniques knowing when and where to use it is key.

Best Hybrid waters

It can be no surprise that lakes with plenty of Carp in them are the best places to fish a Hybrid. Commercially run waters and some fishing clubs have well stocked Carp lakes used for match fishing, which a Hybrid feeder can take full advantage of.

Whenever possible, research the water to find out where the hot spots are. Go online and search for match results from that water. Angling forums can be another good source of unbiased information. Ask an employee, water bailiff or other anglers at the lake. Ultimately, fishing the place, watching the water, watching what other people do will give you first hand local knowledge.

The type of waters where you might struggle with a Hybrid feeder are natural waters. These are very unlikely to have a large head of Carp, but may well have vast numbers of silvers (Roach, Rudd etc.) which can demolish a feeder in literally five minutes. Natural waters and estate lakes are very likely to have a layer of soft silt on the bottom, into which a feeder can sink out of sight.

At most places I have fished, the Carp patrol the margins in the mornings and evenings, but prefer the middle in the day. Many commercial and some club operated fisheries, exploit this behaviour by digging lakes with islands in the middle for anglers to fish against. Alternatively, a long narrow lake is dug which looks like a short stretch of canal, or a snake lake, which is of uniform width but twists and turns. Fished from only one side, snake and canal lakes offer an undisturbed bank for the Carp to patrol along. With all the noise and disturbance of anglers on one side, the Carp remain tight against the quiet bank. On these types of waters, a narrow channel or with an island, the Hybrid/Banjo feeders are designed to be cast as tight as possible under the far bank. Safe in the knowledge that the Carp will be there.

Lake design can be used to create areas fish prefer and give the angler the very best chance of catching, but it's up to the individual angler to make the most of these places. There are of course many lakes that don't have an island. Lakes of all shapes, sizes and depths with no obvious feature to fish against. The fish may still go from margin to middle and back in a day, but there will be no obvious place to drop your feeder.

Hybrid/Banjo techniques

All coarse fishing methods are about finding the fish, getting them to feed and hooking a few while they eat. Hybrid and Banjo feeders are designed to catch one fish at a time. They are the catching part of fishing, but they only play a small part in the feeding aspect.

When the Carp are actively searching for food, especially when there is competition for food from other Carp in the lake. Limiting the amount of feed in the swim can be advantageous. Ironically, feeding too much and attracting too many fish into the swim can be counter productive. Having too many fish in the swim can cause them to dart about and squabble over the food.

With all the activity, the feed and hook bait can be washed out of the feeder. Line bites and foul hooked fish can become a real problem. In an ideal world the amount of feed should be carefully controlled to attract some fish, but not too many.

Hybrid and Banjo feeders are designed for use with small or micro pellets as the feed. Most fish will eat micro pellets, including vast numbers of silver fish that are likely to share the lake. Silvers are usually the first to find the feeder. Small twitches of the rod tip will indicate their presence as they demolish your carefully prepared feeder. After a time the rod tip stops twitching, don't be fooled into thinking that the tiddlers have given up and that the next bite will be a Carp. No, a quiet tip means the feeder is empty!

Silvers can empty a feeder in less than ten minutes, so when the tip goes quiet it's a sure sign it's time to reel in and reload the feeder. Without feed in the feeder, the chances of catching a Carp is greatly reduced, the feeder must have some feed in it at all times.

Carp in the vicinity will eventually be attracted to your swim, not only by the activity of the silvers, but also by the regular splash of a freshly filled feeder entering the water. When the Carp arrive, the twitching of the rod tip will change. No longer the constant quivering of the silver fish, but instead the pulls of line bites as Carp move around the swim.

Now the Carp are in the swim it is time to catch as many as possible. The self hooking nature of the trap means when a fish is hooked, the rod tip will pull round hard. For as long as the fish stay, it should just be a matter of catching one-a-chuck.

Eventually the Carp will move off, either because too many have been hauled out or all in the immediate area have been caught. You will know because the bites will slow and the silvers will return. Once again resume casting regularly and watching for the Carp.

On some venues and at times when the fish are receptive, the sound of loose pellets pinged over the top can attract Carp into the swim. Introducing extra feed in this way has to be done cautiously, the purpose is to attract the fish with the noise of the feed hitting the surface. The Carp learn that this is free food and the dinner bell is ringing. The one thing to avoid is to attract too many fish, so feed very sparingly with two or three noisy, splashy 8mm pellets every 30 seconds to a minute. If this fails to draw the fish into your swim, try casting to another place. Trying a new swim which might be just two yards from where you were, can transform the day, whether you have been catching or not. The practice of casting around for a bite can be invaluable in the cold of winter when Carp gather together in tight shoals.

Bites and indications

Proper bites are bold and unmistakable. The self-hooking nature of flatbed feeders and the subsequent realisation by the fish, will cause any fish that falls for the trap to bolt pulling the rod tip around hard.

Another useful indication is a line bite. This is where a fish brushes against the mainline as it moves around the swim. The rod tip will pull slowly for a few inches then suddenly spring back as the line slips off the fish's body. Line bites indicate the presence of fish in the area, so be ready for action.

A few big line bites may be the first signs of bigger fish entering the swim. If the swim becomes overrun with Carp, they can disturb the feeder and produce multiple line bites which can get so bad as to confuse the angler. Glance up from the tip and look at the swim. If there are clouds of mud, swirling or bubbles fizzing at the surface, it's probably safe to assume too many fish. Cut back on the feed by casting less often, let the situation calm down and take control once more.

One other indication to look out for is a drop back bite. This is when a fish gets hooked and bolts directly towards you. The line will immediately go slack and the rod tip straightens. Any time a drop back bite occurs, pick up the rod and reel in. Sometimes you will connect with a fish, but other times the drop back would have been caused by the feeder moving from it's position. Whether you land a fish or if the feeder has moved, you will need to reload and recast.

Method feeder

Method feeders possess the same advantages as all flatbed feeders, tangle free casting and self hooking. What separates them from the rest is how they feed the fish. Their open design allows the feed to spill out around the feeder in a halo. A very different approach from Hybrid's and Banjo's where much of the feed remains in the bowl of the feeder. Size for size, Method feeders can also be loaded with more feed. Their open design and greater capacity makes them indispensable in the spring and summer when the fish are hungry.

There is a large range and variety of baits that can be used with a Method feeder. Many of the bait manufacturers offer a range specifically for flatbed feeders including the Method. Sticky pellets and Method mix groundbaits come in a bewildering variety of flavours, colours and textures.

Using a Method feeder

The whole idea of the method feeder is a simple one, but getting the feed right and loading it on the feeder is the trick. First job is to prepare pellets or method mix groundbait to put on the feeder frame. The feed will also need to stay on during the cast and through the water to the lake bed.

Once on the bottom, the feed breaks down and falls away creating an attractive halo of food with the hookbait right in the middle. This makes a large target for the fish to home in on. If groundbait and or liquid flavours are also used, colour and flavour can spread to pull fish from further away. This leads us to an important aspect of Method feeder fishing, it can be used to feed and attract fish into the swim.

Preparing the feed

Preparing the feed is the first job to do on arrival. With a Method mix groundbait, put the dry powder into a bucket and add a little pond water. Give it a good mix then riddle the groundbait into another bucket. The lumps are the wettest parts of the groundbait. By using a riddle you will break up these wetter lumps and spread them through the rest of the mix. Now you must leave the groundbait to soak for a good 15 minutes.

To prepare pellets, put some into a bait box and just cover them with pond water. Leave to soak for one minute for each millimetre in size. Oily pellets like Halibut take longer, sometimes much longer depending on the brand. Once they have soaked, drain off the excess water and leave to stand for 15 minutes.

Some types of pellets stick together better than others. Micro or small pellets stick together better than the larger pellets. If the pellets you want to use refuse to stick together, then you can add them to some prepared groundbait in a 50/50 mix.

Loading a Method feeder

Place the hook and bait in the bottom of the feeder mould. Fill the mould with feed and press the feeder into the mould frame first. Give the feeder a firm squeeze in the mould then press the underside of the mould to eject the loaded feeder. With pellets it's exactly the same, hook bait in the bottom, feed on top, squeeze the feeder into the mould.

Fig 13: Empty and loaded Method feeders.

As the feeder falls through the water, some of the feed will inevitably be washed off. If the water is more than six feet deep, you may have to double skin the feeder to make sure the hook bait isn't washed off on the way down. Double skinning is simply loading the feeder as normal then adding an extra layer of feed over the top. The skin will then hold the bait in place as the feeder sinks. Skinning can also help if you are being plagued by small fish eating the feed. The extra feed in the skin will allow you to keep the feeder in the swim a few minutes longer.

Feed too wet

Every groundbait and every type of pellet will take a different amount of water. You can always add more water to groundbait, or soak pellets a second time if too dry, but once either is too wet, you've got a problem. Not only when loading the feeder, but also how the feed behaves in the water.

If groundbait or pellets are sticking to the inside of the feeder mould, they are too wet. Pellets can be mixed with groundbait to get around the problem. With groundbait that is too wet there are various tricks you can try, like putting the mould inside a polythene bag then loading the feeder on top. Or try wetting the mould first, or add more dry mix to groundbait. The trick I prefer to use is to smear a little Hemp oil on the inside of the mould, this I find lasts two or three loads before I have to put more on.

Feeding approach

Hybrid and Banjo feeders are designed with Carp as the target fish, but the Method has proven to be less selective when other species are present. Broadening the species of target fish in a session usually yields a greater number of fish caught overall.

The amount of feed introduced can be controlled when loading a Method feeder, or by how often a loaded feeder is cast to the swim. To get some feed on the bottom to kick start the swim involves nothing more than reloading and casting in short order. After the initial baiting, reload and cast the feeder at regular intervals, perhaps every ten to fifteen minutes. Reloading at regular intervals is an easy way to monitor the amount of feed introduced. Many anglers use a stopwatch to accurately follow a feeding routine. If this sounds a bit too formal, more like work than pleasure, I would say remember the feeder is empty when the rod tip stops quivering, or if you don't catch any fish. If nothing else, recast now and then to improve your chances. Double skinning is a good way of boosting the amount of feed mid session if things go a bit quiet.

A large amount of feed may be required in warm conditions to keep the fish coming, but In the cold the exact opposite is true. In winter when an angler can only reasonably expect to catch a few fish, introducing a feeder full of pellets on each cast can be too much. The fish quickly eat their fill and stop feeding. When it's cold, the trick is to reduce the amount of feed by loading the feeder with just groundbait. It will attract the fish, but the only substantial item of food they will find is the hookbait.

Changing the percentage of groundbait to pellets is yet another method of controlling the amount of feed.

The preferred groundbaits for Carp are the fishmeal and sweet fishmeal mixes, especially on commercials. Do not use a groundbait that has crushed hemp as one of it's ingredients. Crushed Hemp is an active ingredient, which means particles will float up and sink back down causing a column of particles and oil that silvers find attractive. More importantly though, the Carp can also be attracted up in the water away from the Method feeder on the bottom.

As with all fishing, the key to catching more fish on the Method is to use the right feed in the right amounts. When the fish have less of an appetite overfeeding them will kill the swim. In cold conditions when the fish are lethargic, on hot days when the oxygen levels drop in the water, a small amount of feed will better suit the circumstances. At the other end of the scale when the fish are "having it", Carp especially can get through a great deal of feed. The point is to avoid overfeeding, but at the same time to feed enough to keep them coming; Definitely not easy.

The initial baiting to start the swim is perhaps the hardest, there is no way of knowing what mood the fish are in, or if there are any fish in front of you. The only thing to do is take an educated guess.

Winter Method feeder fishing

Fish do not actively look to feed when the weather is cold and water temperature is low. They shoal together in tight groups in areas they find most comfortable. My usual approach in the cold is to hunt for the fish. Load a micro feeder with micro pellets and cast to an area. Leave the feeder in for exactly ten minutes. If there are no signs of fish, it is safe to assume there are no fish there. On the next cast land the feeder a couple of yards from the first spot. Once again watch the tip closely for ten minutes. Moving along an island one cast at a time, or across open water looking for signs of fish. The tip will twitch or slow line bites will reveal the location of the shoaled fish.

A micro feeder full of feed put out for the Carp can quickly be picked clean by tiddlers. Recast at regular intervals until eventually a Carp is lured in, resulting in a full blooded pull on the tip.

Quick change feeders

The Hybrid/Banjo feeders contain most of the feed within the bowl of the feeder, Method feeders can carry a greater quantity and different varieties of feed which are allowed to spread. These two types of flatbed feeder offer two very different feeding options. This is important because how the swim is fed has the biggest impact on how well you do. Get the feeding right and you will catch more fish, it's that simple.

Controlling the amount of feed introduced has been made much easier by tackle manufacturers producing interchangeable feeder bodies.

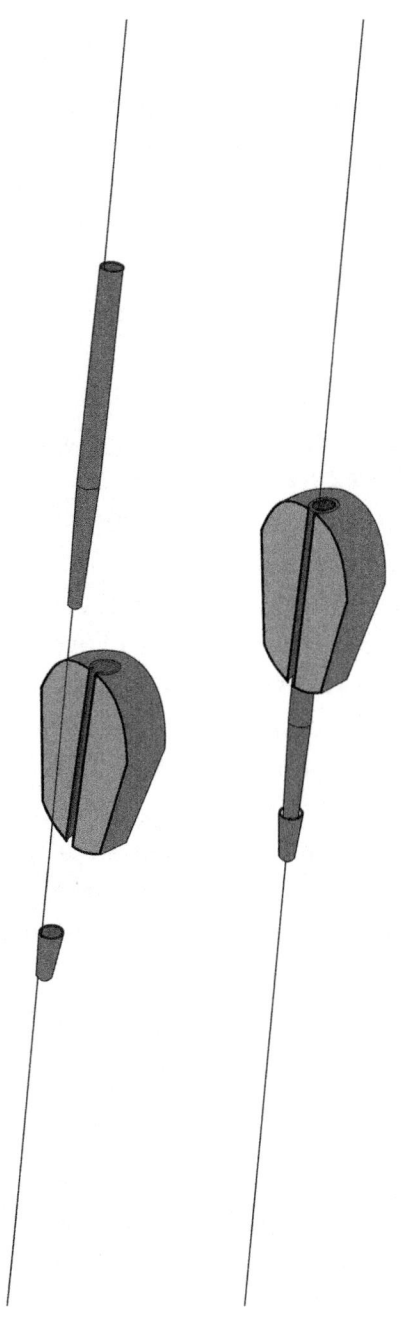

Fig 14: Interchangeable feeder system.

For years flatbed feeders were made as a single unit. If the angler wanted to change approach mid session, either a second rod was needed or they had to break down and retie the rig with a different feeder. Most anglers, especially pleasure anglers, felt disinclined to do this, many sessions are fished with only one rig. Being able to swap the feeder body without breaking down has allowed anglers to quickly change method, presentation and feed quantity on the fly.

Begin with three or four loaded Method feeders in quick order. Cast out and leave the feeder in for just a couple of minutes to allow the feed to soften. Jerk the feeder off the bottom to wash any remaining feed off in the swim. Once a little bait is on the bottom, change to a Hybrid and begin fishing. If the tip reports the attention of small fish at the feeder, recast every ten minutes to ensure the Hybrid always has some feed in it.

Eventually some Carp will move into the swim attracted by the feed on the bottom. At this point expect some of them to take the bait, but this won't last. The Hybrid is not good at feeding the shoal of Carp in the swim, it will be necessary to top up the feed. A dropping catch rate or the return of the small fish is a good indication that more feed is needed.

Additional bait can be catapulted in over the top, but if the water is more than a few feet deep, the loose feed will cause the Carp to come up in the water, taking them away from the feeder. In deeper water change to a Method and feed three or four feeders full again, then swap back to the Hybrid in readiness of the Carps return.

An alternative to keep swapping feeders is to have a second rod set up with a feeding rig. In this case a powerful rod, strong line with a big cage feeder on the end. A big cage feeder can feed more in one cast than a Method feeder. It may only be necessary to cast once or twice to get the same effect.

Hook baits

Use the same hook baits with a Method as with a Hybrid/Banjo feeder, generally an 8mm pellet, boilie or Wafter on a size 12 hook. Be aware that fish can get smart to a bait, but also they can be very picky. If you cannot get any bites when there is evidence of fish in the swim, change the hook bait. A slow day can be turned into a red letter day by simply changing the bait, so always keep an open mind.

Pellet feeders

There are three main reasons to use a pellet feeder. First is to control the amount of feed in a swim. Pellet feeders carry less feed than any other flatbed feeder, this is particularly useful when too much feed has been introduced and the fish have got overly excited. Second scenario is deep water. By design feed pellets will stay in a pellet feeder right to the bottom, in fact it's not unusual to find the feeder half full on retrieval. Lastly, pellet feeders are great in the winter, once again because they carry only a small amount of feed.

How pellet feeders work

Flatbed pellet feeders have only one open end (Fig.15). Feed pellets are loaded to fill most of the feeder, leaving perhaps one quarter for the hookbait and a last layer of pellets to hold it in. Just as with the other flatbed feeders, the pellet feeder is self hooking. Hook links are commonly 2 to 4 inches long with four inches being the norm. Hair rigged bait of 6mm to 8mm in size either banded or spiked.

On the lake bed, the pellets in the front fall away to present the hookbait in the mouth of the feeder. Carp have no choice but to suck at the front of the feeder to get the pellets. Inevitably the hook bait is sucked up along with the pellets and the fish self hooks.

Preparing the pellets

Pellet preparation is slightly different for use in a pellet feeder. The pellets need to be dryer to ensure they absorb enough water to expand and push out the pellets in the front of the feeder. Immerse micro feed pellets in pond water for half the usual amount of time. Instead of one minute for each millimetre of pellet diameter, dip for 30 seconds per millimetre. Groundbait may be used as a binder and attractor with 25% groundbait to 75% pellets being a good mix. Dampen groundbait enough to bind, but keep it on the dry side.

Loading a pellet feeder

Scoop prepared pellets into the feeder until it's three quarters full and firmly press the pellets down. Place the hookbait in the mouth of the feeder and finish filling the feeder to the top. Press this last layer of pellets using medium pressure. Use the same procedure whether groundbait is used or not.

Some anglers prefer to bury the hook link line inside the feeder as the feed is loaded, which will hold the hook close to the mouth of the feeder. This idea relies on the feed being loose enough in the feeder to pull free as the fish is feeding. If the feed is tight in the feeder, or does not break down correctly, the hook link line may remain inside the feeder. Getting the feed just right can be difficult. Personally I only use this method when I believe the fish are evading the hookbait. The usual method is to leave the hook link line outside the feeder with just the hook and bait under the top layer of feed. If the fish are suspected of avoiding the hook, or if the hook is being washed away from the front of the feeder, use a shorter hook link perhaps as short as two inches. It doesn't matter if the feeder is not fully emptying as the hook will remain very close to the mouth of the feeder.

Using a pellet feeder

Just as with the other flatbed feeders, a pellet feeder is a tangle free, self hooking rig which is easy to set up, cast and use. The real difference is in feeding and presentation. Pellet feeders by design keep the hookbait close to the free offering increasing the odds of a bite.

On heavily fished waters where the Carp get wise, pellet feeders offer a different presentation which can improve your catches while others look on with envy.

Pellet feeders are not particularly good at feeding a swim. A better approach is to use a Method or cage feeder to kick start or top-up a swim, then use the pellet feeder over the top. Loose feed can also be pinged in to attract fish to the area, just don't over do it and bring the fish up in the water.

Winter is another good time to employ a pellet feeder. Casting around to find the Carp and using it to feed small amounts, keeps the fish coming in the same way as a micro feeder. Controlling the feed and reacting to how the fish respond has always been the key to fishing, no matter when, no matter where.

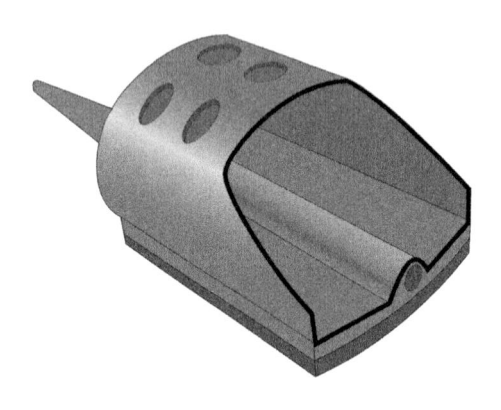

Fig 15: Pellet feeder.

Open End Feeders

Long before flatbed feeders became popular, open end feeders were a revolution on the match fishing scene. Open end feeders literally changed the way anglers fished. A static bait presented on the bottom along with feed proved to be much better at catching bags of Bream and Roach than the float, much to the disgust of the traditional anglers. Feeder fishing has now matured into a truly accepted tactic for catching fish. Between them, the different types of feeder will allow an angler to fish on any water for almost any species of fish.

The best way to attract and hold fish in your swim, is as always, to give them some food. Throwing or catapulting loose feed works well on a lake up to about twenty yards, but the further out you fish, the more difficult it becomes. Feeding distance can be doubled by using loose feed bound in groundbait, but there is a limit as to how far a ball of groundbait can be thrown accurately.

A river presents a different set of problems, the worst of which is knowing exactly where loose feed has landed on the river bed. In a strong flow, light baits such as maggots can be swept a long way downstream before they touch bottom, if at all. A swim feeder ensures the feed will always land next to the hook bait, even at distance or in a flow.

Feeders can be used to carry groundbait, particles, pellets, maggots or a combination of feed. The whole idea behind a feeder is to efficiently and accurately deposit feed along with the hook bait, whatever the circumstances.

The quantity of feed introduced on each cast is simply controlled by the size of the feeder or the frequency of cast. The rate of feed released can be regulated by either the design of the feeder, or the type of feed.

Rods and reels

Feeder fishing is the preferred method for most anglers when the fish are more than 20m from the bank. Much further than this and seeing a float or accurately feeding by hand become increasingly more difficult. With a reasonably well practised casting technique, the majority of anglers can fish effectively up to 50m, beyond this distance is usually the domain of the professional angler. A person who has spent thousands of hours on the bank and can repeatedly cast over 50m to an area the size of a small dining table. For the rest of us, feeder fishing means dropping a line somewhere between 20m and 50m. Even if you are looking out over the vast expense of a reservoir, chances are fish will be found within 50m of the bank. River fishing is a different matter. It would be unusual and almost certainly unnecessary to cast any great distance fishing a river. What does matter is how much weight is needed to hold the bottom.

I imagine for most angling enthusiasts two feeder rods will cover most venues. Firstly a 10ft (3m) rod with an upper casting weight of 40g paired with a 4000 reel, which should cover stillwater casting up to 30m and a river with a medium flow. The second rod might be 11ft (3.3m) in length with a maximum casting weight of 60g also paired with a 4000 reel, allowing a comfortable cast of 50m with a 50g weight.

Fishing line

Monofilament and braid are the two types of main line most suited to feeder fishing. Mono because it has an amount of stretch and braid because it doesn't.

The stretch in mono is useful to help absorb the shock of casting a heavy feeder. It also lessens the chance of a hook pull in the final stages of playing a fish close to the net.

Braided lines having zero stretch offering a very direct connection to the rig. Bites are more immediate and positive even when the rig is at some distance. Casting range is also further with a braid main line because of it's smaller diameter. The payoff with using low stretch braid as the main line is that it does not give at all while playing a fish. Care must be taken, especially with Bream, to use correctly balanced tackle and a soft clutch to prevent hook pulls. Conversely, the payoff with mono is too much stretch when playing a fish. At a distance mono can feel as if the fish is on elastic! The elasticity of monofilament only really becomes a concern when fishing beyond 30m to 35m.

A reel loaded with 0.10mm (13lb) braid and a 10lb or 12lb monofilament leader tied on the end gives the best of both worlds. The braid improves casting and bite registration, while the mono provides some shock absorption when casting and playing a fish.

A shock leader should be long enough to have three or four turns of mono around the spool, then up the rod through the rings and down to the rig. This length of leader line ensures only the mono is involved in the initial strain of casting.

I said earlier that balanced tackle and a soft clutch can go a long way to reducing hook pulls. To save your fingers from deep cuts, it is important to tighten the clutch before casting. A heavy feeder can cause a lightly set clutch to slip just as the rod loads. If the clutch should slip while casting, the line will cut your finger as it slips. Always tighten the clutch before casting a long way, then loosen it by the same amount after the cast.

Ready made tapered shock leaders are available. The thin end is tied to the braid to allow a smaller knot. The rig is tied to the thick end. Use an Albright knot to attach either a tapered or straight leader to a braided main line.

One final thing to mention about braid is that some fisheries have banned it's use. Please check local or fishery rules before setting up.

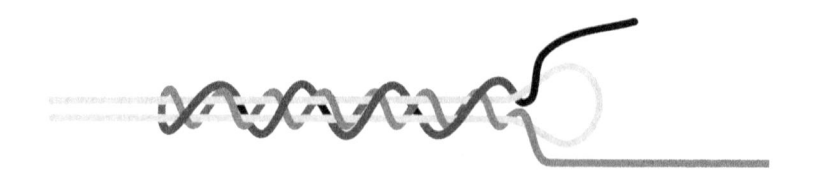

Fig 16: Albright knot.

Essential rigs

Over time an angler will collect a range of feeder rods and reels to suit all the different lakes and rivers he fishes. It may take years to assemble enough equipment to properly fish at close range on a lake, or long range on a reservoir and all the infinitely variable conditions of running water. The one constant throughout will be the method of bite indication; a quiver tip.

In modern feeder fishing, the quiver tip rod, or more commonly called the feeder rod has become king. Swing tip rods were once all the rage, but are very rarely seen today. Other methods including the more sensitive touch ledgering and bobbin type bite indicators used in Carp fishing don't lend themselves to feeder fishing. Unless otherwise stated, assume all the rigs and methods we are about to discuss, are described with a feeder rod in mind.

All feeder fishing rigs rely on one of two ways of indicating a bite. Either a fish pulls on the line causing the rod tip to pull round. Or the feeder is disturbed, slackening the line causing a drop-back bite where the rod tip springs straight.

There are two essential rigs on which all feeder fishing rigs are based. The running rig and the helicopter rig. These two rig types can be used on all stillwater fisheries no matter what size. River fishing really only needs the running rig. Both rigs are capable of producing either kind of bite, with other factors deciding which rig is best on the day.

The running rig

In feeder fishing a running rig is a setup where the feeder (the weight) is not tied to the main line. In other words the feeder is not fixed, it is able to slide along the line. This is done for fish safety. Imagine while playing a fish the main line was to snap or be cut by a sharp object beneath the surface. The fish would remain hooked to the rig and tethered to the weight of the feeder. The fish may be able to shed the hook leaving the rig behind, but if it can't, it could eventually kill the fish. If the main line were to break using a running rig, the feeder will slide down and off the broken line attached to the hooked fish. Although the fish might still have a length of line trailing behind, the fish is not tethered to a heavy weight and stands a much better chance of survival.

In reality fish are surprisingly good at removing hooks from their mouths, but we as anglers must do everything possible to keep fish safe. To this end, most fisheries have banned the use of fixed rigs and I too do not recommend the use of unsafe rigs.

Keep it simple

Much is written about rigs in the angling press and on the internet giving the impression that rigs are the be all and end all of fishing. This is simply not true. A feeder rig is used to place a feeder full of free offerings close to the hookbait in an area where we feel the fish might be. With luck, some fish will happen upon the food and take the bait. It does not matter in any way which rig got the bait to where the fish can find it, it only matters that it did. When a fish takes the hookbait the rig may then play a part in causing a bite, something which I will expand upon later. For now, let's look at how to tie a good, simple, reliable running rig.

The idea with a running rig is for the weight, a feeder in this case, to slide freely up and down the line. Fish safety of course, but also for a fish pulling on the line to show at the rod tip.

Despite it's supposed invisibility under water, I don't like to use fluorocarbon because it has very little stretch. That's not to say you cannot use fluorocarbon, I just prefer not to. I like to tie all my feeder rigs with monofilament lines.

Tying the basic running rig

Some feeders have a swivel built in and some just have a ring or loop. In any event, it is usually desirable to be able to change the feeder without the need to break the whole rig down.

Thread a snap link swivel or a proper feeder bead and snap link on the line. A snap link allows the feeder to be changed to a different weight or different design mid session if needed.

Next on the line is a line stop, which is a tight fitting silicone bead. Line stops are supplied on a loop of thin wire. To get a stop onto the line, thread the line through the wire loop and simply pull the bead across and onto the fishing line.

To help reduce tangles on the cast, a stiffer section of line called a "Twizzled boom" is needed next down the line below the feeder.

Double the line and tie a figure-of-eight loop knot leaving a long 12 inch tail. Hold the main line in one hand and the end of the tail in the other. Twisting both the line and tail end in opposite directions will cause the lines to wrap around each other creating a Twizzled section. Pulling the line apart and then bringing them back together will make the twists in the Twizzle tighter if needed. Make an 8 inch long Twizzled section. Tie a double overhand knot to secure the Twizzled section at 6 inches long. Slide the line stop down until it touches the top of the Twizzled boom.

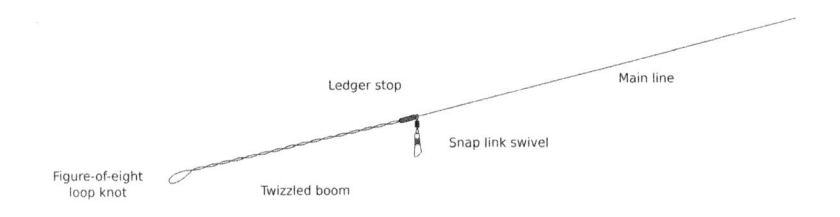

Fig 17: Running rig without hook link or feeder.

Looking at the finished rig, there is a loop at the end which is used to connect the hook link. Above the loop is a 6 inch Twizzled boom with a line stop tight against the top knot. Finally above the line stop is the free running snap link swivel or feeder link bead.

When the weight of a feeder is hanging on the line, the line stop causes the Twizzled boom to kick out away from the feeder. This in turn holds the hook link out of harm's way greatly reducing tangles on the cast and in the air. Some anglers prefer to use one or two No.8 Stotz instead of a line stop above the Twizzled boom, because they offer a flat right angle to the feeder link.

Clip on a feeder and loop-to-loop connect a hook link to make the rig ready for use.

Fig 18: Complete feeder rig with hook link and feeder.

How the running rig works

At the most basic level, when a fish takes the hook bait and swims away it pulls the line through the feeder link causing the rod tip to pull towards the lake. The further the fish swims the further round the rod tip moves, perhaps to a point where the rod is pulled off the rests. Positive unmissable bites like this can and do happen, but this perfect bite definitely does not happen every time.

For many new to fishing, it is assumed the running rig depends on the feeder staying put on the bottom while the line is pulled through by the fish. Straight away this assumes the fish will swim away in the first place, and swim directly away from the anglers position on the bank.

If the fish swims in any other direction, especially up in the water or towards the bank, the line will not pull through the feeder as easily. The answer is not to use a feeder heavy enough to hold bottom come what may, the answer is to allow the feeder to move.

While waiting for a bite, the line is held tight from the feeder to the rod tip. If a fish pulls directly on the line the rod tip will move towards the water. If the feeder is dislodged because the fish has moved in some other direction, the tension on the tip is immediately released causing the rod tip to spring back. Drop-back bites are very common, in fact you are more likely to see a drop back-bite than a straight pull with this rig. It does not matter if the tip is pulled round or springs back, it's movement indicates the presence of a fish either way.

Unfortunately, a quiver tip can only move in two directions, unlike a float which can indicate a bite in any one of six. Yet a quiver tip can tell us much.

Running rig bites

A quiver tip can only pull round or spring back straight when something under the water acts upon the rig. There are many things that we cannot see from the bank that can cause an indication at the rod tip. Detritus washed downstream on a river for example, can catch on the line slowly pulling the tip round. If enough debris builds up, the tip will be pulled right round making the rig unfishable. It is usually quite obvious when debris has caught the line, the only option is to reel in to clear the line. Anytime the tip is slowly pulled round and stays round is cause to suspect something is fouling the line, reel in and check.

A similar and more common indication is for the tip to slowly pull round to suddenly spring back to it's original position. Note I say to it's original position.

This indicates something under the water has brushed past the line. Large, positive line bites like this, may indicate some fish are near or around the feeder. The fact that the rod tip has returned to it's starting position means that the feeder has not been disturbed and has not moved on the lake bed.

Another type of line bite is a quick tug on the tip, which once again returns to where it was. These quick jabs are smaller fish darting around bumping into the line as they go. They may not be tiny fish. An excited shoal of 12oz Roach can easily produce a series of quick line bites betraying their presence in the swim.

Roach are often the first fish to find a freshly baited swim, to see line bites from them is a good sign. Their excitement in discovering free food just laying there for the taking will help to attract other fish to the spot. All we have to do is keep feeding them.

Once Roach settle and begin to feed, the quick jerks of line bites give way to an entirely different and distinctive indication. Small twitches that turn into trembles and quivers are the indications we want. These are the bites of Roach. River Roach in particular give themselves away with a quivering bite. But, and it's a big but, should you strike at a quiver?

Feeder fishing does not lend itself to fast striking because of the weight of the feeder and water resistance it offers. A fast strike can break the line. Wait for Roach to hook themselves, indicated by the non stop rattling of the tip. Pick the rod up and "pull" into the fish with a slow deliberate action, avoiding snatching at it.

The final type of bite is the easiest to read, the one where the tip just pulls round after a couple of knocks, or pulls round after a drop back bite. Bream are nearly always the cause of these slow positive bites and they come about because they have self hooked. Keep calm and just pick the rod up without striking and play the fish.

When and where to use the running rig

The running rig is a general purpose rig which can be used on a variety of waters, so long as the lake or river bed is firm. The contents of a feeder need to disperse and remain on top of the substrate where the fish can find it. Dropping any feeder rig into a swim with a soft silt bottom will greatly reduce it's effectiveness. Before setting up cast a bomb around the area to find a patch of bottom where the feeder will not sink.

Ideal for plastic feeders, cage feeders, maggot feeders and feeders with side weights, the running rig is best used at a fairly close range of up to 50m. On stillwaters a cast could be much greater which is where the limits of the running rig are met. The rig is not designed to cast a very long way, the helicopter rig is much better suited to distance.

The rig may offer little resistance to a taking fish, assuming the fish swims directly away from the angler. If the fish goes in any other direction it will feel something. This is not a problem. More often than not we want the rig to offer some resistance, it is this resistance that can pull on the hook link and cause the hook to prick the fish's mouth. Once hooked in this way, a positive bite will result at the tip, either drop back, pull round or both in that order. In fact I would say ignore any little twitches of the tip and wait for a definite bite before picking the rod up.

The running rig lends itself for use in spring and summer when the fish are active and bold in their feeding. Best results come from dropping it into any area of clean, firm lake bed where a feeder can deposit it's payload effectively. I also favour the running rig for fishing rivers. Most rivers have a bed scoured clean every winter by the floods making them ideal for this rig. River fish are also less likely to have seen much in the way of anglers and their rigs, which means with good presentation, bold bites are the norm.

The feeder link running rig

Not all fish will produce a positive bite when using the simple running rig. Some fish are more cautious or reject the bait if they feel any resistance. A slight variation is needed to reduce the resistance offered by the rig to improve bite registration. In essence, we want the fish to register a bite at the rod tip long before it feels the weight of the feeder.

To add some free movement in the rig, a disconnect between the line and the feeder has to be introduced. This is done by swapping the snap link swivel connecting the feeder, with a feeder link.

Fig 19: Feeder link.

A feeder link is simply a piece of line with an eye at one end and a snap link swivel at the other. Instead of putting the snap link swivel directly onto the main line, it is connected by a piece of line which holds it away from the main line.

By connecting the feeder on the end of an extension, a fish is able to move a few inches pulling on the rod tip before the weight of the feeder is met. A fish pulling on the line directly away from the angler, might pull as much as six inches before the feeder is felt. The rod tip would move by this amount clearly showing the presence of the fish long before the fish becomes suspicious. Clearly this ideal scenario does not happen every time, but unless the fish swims directly at you, there will be some movement in the line before the feeder is reached.

Tying the feeder link running rig

As this rig is a variant of the standard running rig described in detail on page 87. Begin by threading on the feeder link and a line stop. Tie a figure-of-eight loop knot and twizzle a boom above it long enough to hang below the feeder. Slide the line stop down to the top knot of the boom.

Using the feeder link running rig

The feeder link running rig works in the same way and in the same circumstances as the basic running rig. It uses the same plastic feeders, cage feeders and other feeders that have their weight to the side. It is capable of producing pull bites and drop back bites and will self hook if the fish swims far enough to reach the feeder. So what is the point of this rig and why use it?

The fundamental change in adding a feeder link is to allow a fish to move a distance before feeling the weight of the feeder. From the fish's point of view, it feels only a small amount of resistance before reaching the feeder. From the anglers view, the rod tip will twitch and quiver before the fish self hooks. We could view this as just an early warning system before a proper bite, which it is, but this rig is more than that.

It allows us to glean more information from what we can't see. More information allows better decision making. More information allows better management of the fish.

Which rig to use

The basic running rig is primarily a blunt instrument for catching fish, which is ideal when the fish are hungry and actively looking for food in spring and early summer. The fish are recovering from the winter and are either building their strength for spawning, or regaining their strength after spawning. Rising temperatures and the last frost are signs the fish are about to get active, but the season is young there isn't an abundance of natural food yet. At these times the fish are so preoccupied with getting fit that they feed with abandon, these are the days when a blunt instrument of a rig is the best option.

Later in the year lakes and rivers are full of natural food and every angler and his mate are chucking more in. The fish have less competition, no need to search, no need to go hungry, they can take their time to feed to satisfaction. Now the fish are harder to catch, we have to change tactics and part of this is catching what we can, when we can, using a more sensitive rig.

When fish are very hungry, they will compete, fight and struggle to get to an anglers feed. Bites are very positive and unmissable as the fish throw caution to the wind, ideal for the basic rig. At times when the fish are not in strong competition with each other, they are more placid and composed, they become more fussy and discriminating. In times of plenty, the more sensitive feeder link running rig will show every little indication at the tip from half hearted fish.

As the days grow shorter and the evenings get cooler, fish often feed heavier to fatten up before the winter. On warmer autumn days the basic rig may still score over a rig with a link. As the year moves on and temperatures drop, not only do the weed beds die back and natural food becomes scarce, but the fish slow down.

Come the winter as water temperature drops, the cold blooded metabolism of fish slows which makes them lethargic and less hungry. The cold temperatures slow their digestion, which altogether means they do not eat much at all. The last thing an angler wants is to make it any harder for a bite to register when conditions are against catching, it is once again time to use the sensitive feeder link rig.

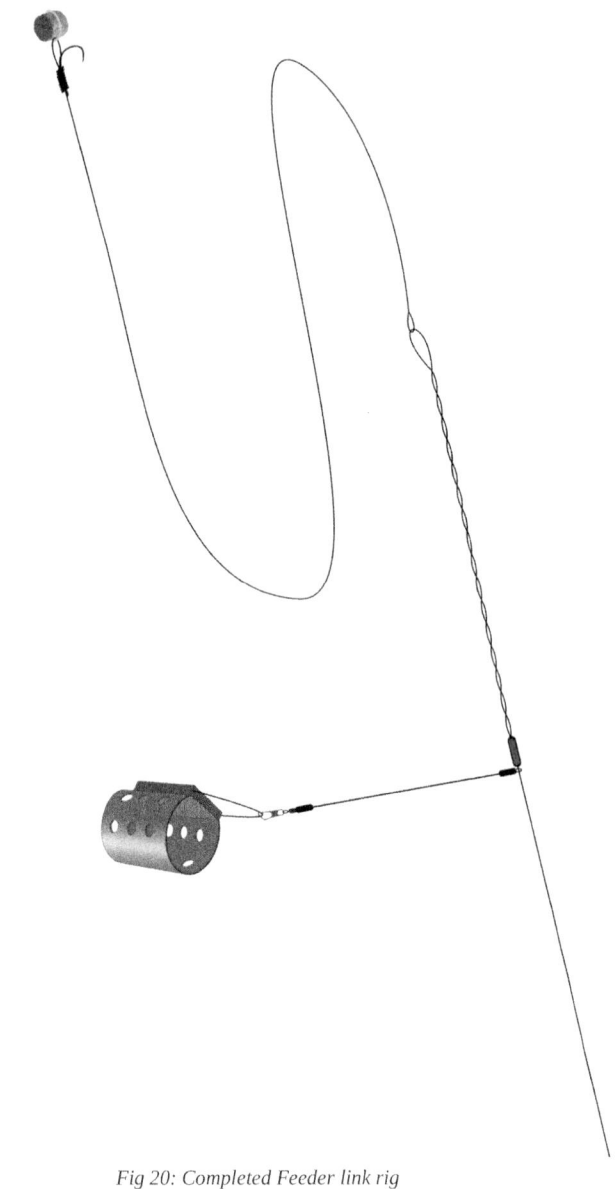

Fig 20: Completed Feeder link rig

The Helicopter rig

In the context of feeder fishing, the Helicopter rig is most suited to long range fishing. The running rig's are ideal for a swim less than 40m and river fishing, but beyond 50m the Helicopter is the best choice.

Tying the Helicopter rig

The casting weight (the feeder) is placed right at the end of the line of a Helicopter rig. The leading position of the feeder not only reduces tangles, but also makes the rig more streamlined and stable in the air. A range of feeder designs have been developed with their weights in the front, rather than on the side, to take full advantage of being on the end of the line.

Begin tying the rig by threading the first of two lines stops onto the main line. Follow it with a small or medium size quick change hook link swivel. Then thread the second line stop on and slide the whole assembly up the line out of the way.

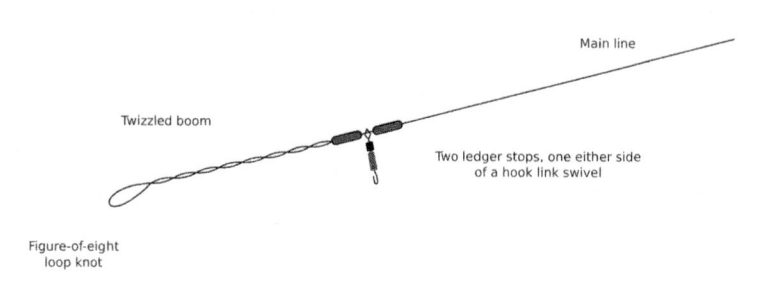

Fig 21: Helicopter rig without hook link or feeder.

Tie a figure-of-eight loop in the end of the main line for a snap link swivel. Either include the snap link within the loop or use the loop to hitch the swivel on later. Either way, leave a long tag end to the knot.

Create a two or three inch twizzled boom with the long tag end and main line. Tie off with a double overhand knot. The twizzled boom serves two purposes. Firstly, it provides a length of stiffer line above the feeder to reduce the risk of tangles. Secondly, when a big fish is hooked the bottom line stop will slide down towards the feeder during the fight. The knot in the top of the twizzled boom will prevent the stop and hook link from getting too close to the feeder. Next clip on a feeder and lastly attach a hook link to the quick change swivel.

Slide the line stops down to between 6 and 8 inches above the feeder. Leave a small gap between the two line stops to allow the hook link swivel to freely rotate on the line. This allows the hook link to "helicopter" on casting rather than wrapping around the main line.

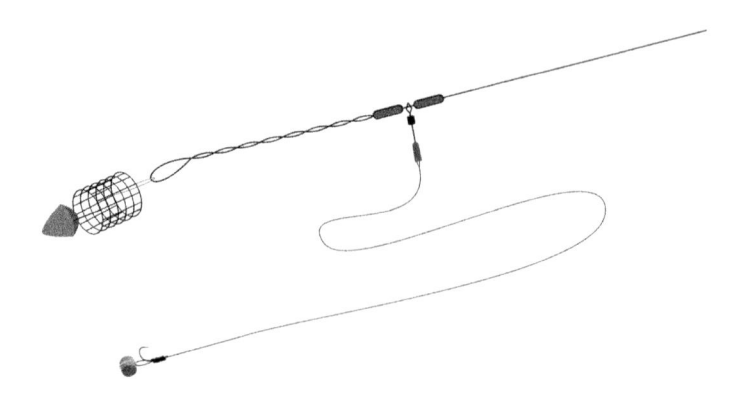

Fig 22: Complete Helicopter rig.

Using the Helicopter rig

The Helicopter rig is acclaimed for it's ability to cast further with an uncanny knack of remaining tangle free. For maximum distance, dedicated "weight forward" feeders have been developed to work with the Helicopter rig, which we will look at later.

Because the feeder is directly tied to the main line, there is a risk of fish becoming tethered in the event of a line break. It is vitally important that the hook link is weaker than the main line. The hook link then becomes the weakest link which will break first if snagged. In addition to this, the stop above the hook link should be able to slide off the main line. The use of split shots or some other fixed stop is frowned upon and often outlawed, so remember to check the fishery rules before fishing.

Helicopter rig bites

There are two common bites seen with a Helicopter rig, a positive pull or a rattling of the rod tip. Drop back bite can still happen, but are less frequent.

The full blooded pulls are usually caused by a fish self hooking against the feeder. Unlike the running rigs where the line can pull through the feeder, the hook link on the Helicopter is semi fixed. At some point the fish will pull directly against the weight of the feeder causing it to self hook, leading to a proper pull on the rod tip. Bream, Carp or Tench are usually the culprits.

Bites where the tip rattles are usually smaller fish, Roach, Skimmer Bream, Perch and the like. In this instance they self hook against the feeder or the tip of the rod, but are not strong enough to dislodge the heavy feeders used to cast a distance. So they end up hooked, but unable to swim any further than the hook link will let them, resulting in a rattle at the rod tip.

Sliding the line stops and hook link assembly further up the line away from the feeder reduces the bolt effect of the rig, but increases the sensitivity. Conversely, moving the assembly closer to the feeder increases the bolt effect. A happy medium can be found on the day by how well the rig is hooking fish or indicating bites. It is not unusual to move the helicopter assembly several times in a session to get the best from the rig. I like to start each session with the assembly at about eight inches from the feeder with a 24 inch hook link and see how the day goes.

Whichever direction a fish swims will cause a pull on the rod tip, unless it swims directly towards the bank causing a drop back bite. Line bites can still happen and from time to time a fish will unhook itself against the weight of the feeder, but on the whole, look for a decent pull or a consistent rattle as your cue to pick the rod up.

When a bite is indicated, pick the rod up and sweep it back. A quick or violent strike is not needed and may result in a line break. Besides, as soon as the feeder is lifted off the bottom, it's weight will jerk down further setting the hook.

Other rigs

A quick search online will reveal a multitude of other feeder fishing rigs, if anything, too many. It is very easy to get drawn into believing that with the right rig, red letter days will become the norm. Constant searching for one rig, one answer in a subject that is so very holistic will lead nowhere. This is one rabbit hole I recommend you walk right past. The rig is only one component of the mechanism of catching fish, it is important I grant you, but you need to look at the whole. The rig is not a solution on it's own.

I have recommended three rigs which I know work and which I know thousands of other anglers put their faith in. Learn them, get to know them and use them. Confidence in them will free you up to concentrate on what really matters.

Hook links (hooklengths) for all rigs

In my book (this book in fact), a hook link is the piece of line that has a hook at one end and connects to the main line at the other. Many call this line a hooklength. For the sake of clarity and to avoid any confusion when I refer to how long a hooklength length is, I call them hook links.

The length, line diameter, line suppleness and the style of hook used in a hook link play an important role in how a hook bait is presented to the fish. Presentation has always been associated with float fishing, but it is every bit as important in feeder fishing. The type of feeder or rig used has little effect on how the hook link behaves. This is why I believe these things need to be contemplated separately when setting up and fishing. Once in the water, all components from the hook to the angler on the bank must be balanced and work in unison.

Thought should be given as to how the hook link will behave as the rig hits the water, sinks to the bottom and how it behaves once laying on the bottom. Imagine a scenario fishing in six feet of water.

You suspect the fish are sitting in mid water at a depth of three feet. The hook and bait will sink past the fish and lay on the bottom with a hook link of 12 inches. The fish might realise you have provided some free offering and drop down to investigate, but if a 36 inch hook link with a slow sinking bait is used, the feeder will hit bottom with the hook bait still up in the water at the same level as the fish. As the hook bait sinks, one or more fish will see the bait and either take it on the drop, or better still, follow it down.

The angling press, angling bloggers and others are often misleading in suggesting there is an optimum length for a hook link. Commonly 30cm for Carp and 50cm for Bream are stated. In my opinion, these are only good lengths to begin a session with. Only once fishing begins and a few fish are caught can the hook link length be properly determined.

Landing a few fish and noting where in the mouth they are hooked is perhaps the best evidence. A long hook link will allow the fish more leeway in deciding whether or not to take the hook bait. If the hook link is too long, the fish has the time to swallow the hook completely before a bite is indicated. On the other hand, a longer hook link might be needed if the fish are pulling off the hook as they are played, or found to have the hook just catching in the lip. When fish are only just hooked, a little more leeway should be given by lengthening the hook link. Ideally, fish that are landed are securely hooked inside the mouth with the eye or spade of the hook at the entrance.

Examining landed fish for clues can only happen if a few are caught. Ironically, it may be necessary to get the hook link correct before any fish can be hooked and landed. Adopting a standard hook link length to begin each session makes sense, after all you have to start somewhere. I like to start with a 24 inch hook link and fish for at least 20 minutes. If no bites are forthcoming, but line bites are seen indicating the presence of fish, I suspect the hook link. If no line bites are seen over that time, I assume the fish have yet to arrive and keep fishing. Although continuing to fish does not mean just sitting there in the hope of the fish turning up. An effort must be made to attract some fish to the area. Recast at regular intervals to top up the feed and create some noise to bring the fish in. If this works, line bites will begin to show.

Once fish are definitely in the swim it should only be a matter of time before a fish is hooked. Note how the bite developed and where in the mouth the fish is hooked. Deep hooked suggests a shorter hook link and lip hooked suggests a longer hook link. Hook link length is not the only factor to consider, line diameter and hook size will play a part.

There is no doubt at all that fine supple hook links catch more fish. There is also no doubt that fine light hooks help the bait to behave naturally. That said, there is a limit to how fine lines and hooks can be and still land the average size of fish in front of you. Hook size is also related to the type and size of bait employed.

One last point before I move on. When the fish are hungry and feeding avidly, shorter hook links will catch fish more efficiently.

When the fish are being cautious, a long hook link will give a fish more time and confidence to take the bait.

With any of the rigs we have looked at, hook links of anywhere from 30cm to 120cm could be needed no matter where you are fishing.

Feeders

The three rigs described will work with the dozen or so feeders we are about to look at. Which feeder to use and with which rig is suggested by the conditions (depth, flow, distance, etc.) at the fishery on the day. The main purpose of the feeder is not only to provide weight to cast with, but also to deposit feed in the right place in the desired way.

The design of a feeder will often indicate it's best use. For example, a plastic feeder will release feed more slowly than a cage feeder. A cage feeder has a very open design to allow the feed to escape easily. When fishing a deep swim, a cage feeder could empty as it sinks through the water, arriving empty with all the groundbait suspended in the water column and the loose feed scattered around. A feeder with fewer holes, like a plastic feeder, is going to carry more feed to the bottom and deposit it closer to the hook.

Some feeder designs are associated with a particular method of fishing. Plastic feeders tend to be thought of as a river feeder and cage feeders are associated with stillwaters. On the whole this is true, but not all the time. I will use a cage feeder on a river if conditions call for it, or if I need to feed quickly. Just as I will use a plastic feeder at a lake when I want to be sure the feed is hard on the bottom and not spread through the water column, which might bring the fish up off the bottom.

Two more designs with a particular purpose in mind are the rocket and maggot feeders. Rocket feeders have their weight at one end rather than on the side to enhance casting. Maggot feeders are designed to carry maggots to the bottom where they can escape.

Every feeder was designed with a purpose and promoted with that purpose foremost. For the angler though, the function of a feeder leading to the desired result is far more important than reputation or association with a particular species or venue.

Four essential feeders
Plastic feeder - open end feeder

Feed is held inside a plastic feeder by a plug of groundbait at each end. Once in the water, the groundbait breaks down releasing the feed bait within. Primarily designed for running water or deep water, the open end feeder deposits it's payload of feed on the bottom close to the hook bait.

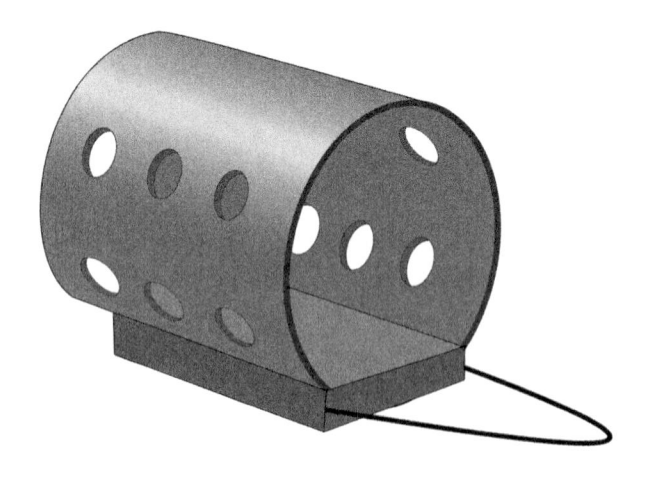

Fig 23: Plastic open end feeder.

As a starting point the hook link should be set so the feed washes down around the hook bait. On a slow river the hook link may be as short as eight inches, but in a faster flow it could be two or more feet. As fish are caught and the hook hold inspected, then the optimum length of the hook link can be determined.

If there is no flow to wash the feeder out, after a short time, move the feeder to cause it to empty. Some anglers are sceptical of doing this because of the danger of spooking the fish, or pulling the hook into debris on the bottom, both of which are possible. On the other hand, moving the feeder away from the feed can be a benefit if the fish are wary of the feeder. For me, I think it's worth trying.

Cage feeder

The wide open mesh of a cage feeder allows feed to quickly escape. Fill with groundbait or liquidised bread with or without feed particles. A dry groundbait mix will explode from the feeder once in the water and the feed will wash out as the feeder sinks. Cage feeders can be used in water up to six feet deep with the right mix.

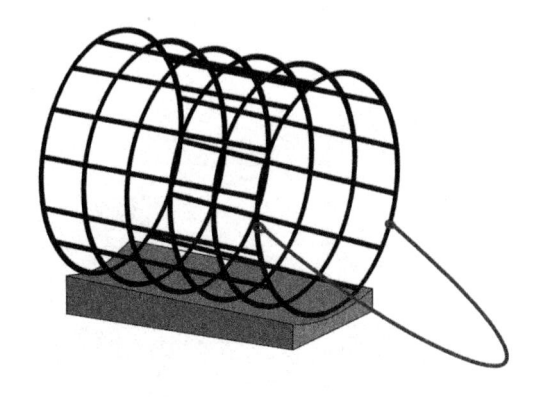

Fig 24: Cage feeder.

Maggot feeder

Maggot feeders, also known as blockend feeders, are a capped cylinder with holes in the sides to allow maggots to escape. The feeder is filled with maggots and quickly cast out. Once on the bottom the maggots will escape creating a halo of free offerings close to the hook baited with a maggot or caster.

The speed at which the maggots escape can be increased by widening the holes in the feeder, or reduced by wrapping electrical tape around the body to block some of the holes.

In a slow river the hook link may be as short as eight inches, but in a faster flow it could be two or more feet. Maggot feeders can be used with the running rig and a long hook link to fish on the drop in stillwater, which is a very effective way of catching Roach, Rudd and skimmers.

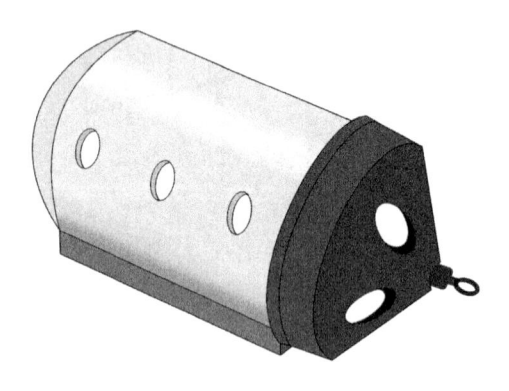

Fig 25: Maggot feeder.

Rocket feeders

Rocket feeders have their weight at one end of the feeder and connect to a helicopter rig at the other. This is a more aerodynamic design allowing rocket feeders to cast much further than plastic and cage feeders with their weight on the side. Both cage and the more closed plastic rocket feeder designs are available. Most effective on a firm bottom where the feeder will fully empty on retrieval.

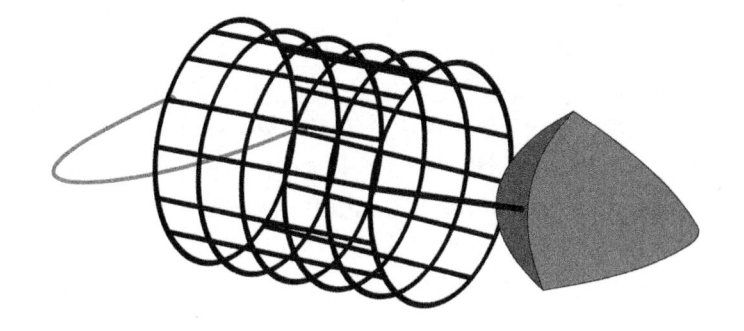

Fig 26: Rocket feeder.

Feeder fishing baits

Feeder fishing is very much a "catch everything" method, it does not discriminate between species. This makes feeder fishing popular with match anglers and pleasure anglers alike, but is a less attractive method to specimen anglers.

Despite the fact feeder fishing can catch any species, it helps when planning a trip to have at least one species in mind. In practice, two species are the mainspring of feeder fishing, Bream and Roach.

Bream are primarily bottom feeders, fishing for Bream opens the door to catch other bottom feeders like Tench and Carp. Roach will often take a bait on the drop or in mid water, as will Rudd, Chub, Dace and Perch. By fishing for either Bream or Roach, or for that matter both, the opportunity to catch other species is also present.

Presentation and the size of bait can add a bias towards one or other fish. A specimen angler will try to exclude small fish by using a large bait. Specimen Beam anglers like to use boilies and big pellets which are too big to be picked up by small silvers for example. Feeder fishing is a method designed to catch as many average sized fish as possible, although a few quality fish are always welcome.

Both Bream and Roach are not fussy and will accept most angling baits from pinkies to pellets and boilies. To fully take advantage of feeder fishing's ability to catch anything that swims, bait choice needs to be appealing to as many species as possible with Bream and Roach as the target fish.

Common, traditional, natural baits are the first choice of the feeder fisherman. Maggots, pinkies, worms, sweetcorn, hemp, but also pellets which are loved by Bream and Roach can be used as loose feed and on the hook.

Groundbaits

The subject of groundbait and groundbait mixes can be complicated and confusing. As a serious angler I have spent many hours wrestling with different makes and mixes and after decades of faffing about I have concluded that simplicity is my preferred option.

European match anglers are renowned for their expertise in groundbait mixtures and baiting patterns and are a good source of information, if this is a subject you wish to pursue. For the vast majority of amateur anglers though, a plain and simple approach will more than satisfy the weekly assault on the local lake.

Bream groundbait

Most fish are opportunists and will feed at any level and any location in a body of water, but they all have their preferred area and method of feeding. Bream primarily feed on the bottom, sucking mouthfuls of mud to filter out particles of food. As shoaling fish they often feed together sometimes in large numbers. The capture of one can often be followed by a flurry of others, especially in the spring. By summer, after the spawning season, Bream are more spread out and big hauls of fish are less likely.

Groundbaits for Bream serve two purposes. Firstly to be the medium to carry particles of feed inside a feeder to the lake or river bed. Secondly, once on the bottom, to break down and release the food along with an attractive taste and smell. To achieve these two goals, a Bream groundbait needs to be of the right consistency and have an attractive flavour.

Although there is an enormous choice of groundbaits on the shelves of any tackle shop, one type of groundbait has established itself as the go-to groundbait for Bream. An inert fishmeal flavoured variety would be my first choice. Summer, winter, river, stillwater matters not, Bream just love fishmeal flavour.

Bream also have a great liking for sweet-tasting foods. Years ago I remember, we used to use simple bread crumbs with a few ground custard cream biscuits added as groundbait. Today, ready-made sweetened fishmeal groundbait can be bought. Alternatively brasum, molasses or betalin can be added to plain fishmeal groundbaits to give it a sweeter taste.

Roach groundbait

Roach are able to feed at any depth in the water column. They can pick out food suspended or swimming in mid water. Pick morsels up off the bottom and insects from the surface. They are truly omnivorous, opportunistic feeders.

To take full advantage of every opportunity, Roach spend much of their time shoaled together swimming at mid water. To attract their attention, an active groundbait is employed. Unlike an inert groundbaits which just sits on the bottom, an active groundbait releases particles that float up creating a cloud of interest from the bottom to the water surface in the path of the Roach. Hemp seeds are the main active ingredient in an active groundbait.

For Roach then, an active cereal (crumb or biscuit) groundbait laced with crushed hemp is just the ticket. Once taken to the lake bed in a feeder, the groundbait will break up releasing not only any free particles of feed included, but also a haze of hemp particles. Often a sort of hemp oil slick will appear on the surface confirming the groundbait is actively working to attract some fish. Personally I like a groundbait with crushed hemp seed and added aniseed flavouring for my Roach fishing.

Preparing groundbait for Bream or Roach

Groundbait for Bream and Roach is mixed in exactly the same way as discussed earlier (page 53). Essentially, add water to dry groundbait including additives in a bucket. Vigorously mix, riddle and stand. This holds true for active Roach groundbaits and can be done on the bank. A Bream groundbait needs a longer preparation. To ensure every particle is damp and will not float up from the bottom, Bream groundbait should be prepared the day before and allowed to soak overnight. Sieve and check the consistency at the water and dampen further if needed. Separate a pint or two of fully prepared groundbait for immediate use in the working bowl, store the rest in a sealed container or plastic bag.

Mix groundbait to the same consistency every time. As the groundbait is carried in the feeder, I don't believe it is necessary to vary the mix too much. Instead, the design of the feeder dictates how or when the feed is released.

Preparing particles

Dead red maggots and floro pinkies are a very effective particle feed to include in the feeder. To prepare them, bag up quantities in freezer food bags, tie the bags off tight to the maggots leaving as little air as possible and put the bags in a freezer for at least 24 hours. It is worth freezing several pints at a time as frozen dead maggots keep for months.

Micro pellets should be soaked if they intend to be used as particle feed. Put some pellets in a bait bowl and cover them in water, add enough water to just cover the pellets. Leave them to soak up all of the water, don't drain them off at all. Caster, dead maggots, corn and hemp should be covered in water to prevent them drying out during the day. Live maggots may die if left in direct sun on a hot day, keep them in shade.

Loading a feeder

It is important to control the quantity of particles included in the groundbait each time the feeder is loaded. The best way to do this is to have plain groundbait in the working bowl and add particles as needed. This could literally mean counting a few dead pinkies or maggots onto the groundbait, then scooping them up with the groundbait as the feeder is loaded.

The quantity of feed particles, whatever they are, should be tightly controlled and regulated by the reaction of the fish.

The procedure is the same for plastic and cage feeders. Push groundbait and feed into the feeder from both sides ensuring all the loose particles are included. Squeeze the groundbait hard enough to remain in the feeder during the cast. If the groundbait refuses to stay in the feeder the mix may be too dry, in which case dampen it a little. If the mix is too sloppy, there is little choice but to mix a fresh batch.

Stillwater feeder fishing

Large lakes and reservoirs offer the best sport to the feeder fisherman. Stillwaters of ten acres or more which have a good proportion of deep water often have a good head of Bream and Roach. Gravel pits are another possibility and reservoirs are a certainty for feeder fishing. Despite a waters size and depth, a feeder rig has the ability to drop on the same spot time after time to create an area of interest to the fish.

Standing on the bank looking at a vast sheet of water can feel intimidating, but you can only fish the small area in front. I like the match anglers approach under these circumstances, make the best of what's in front of you. Try to ignore the vast expanse of water around you and concentrate on the area you can reach, right in front.

Deciding which peg to fish cannot be an exact science on large waters. With the best will in the world, an angler can only ever have a rough idea of where the fish may be. I believe the most we can do is to make a best guess and make the most of what that peg has to offer.

To improve the odds, do as much research as possible, starting with the internet. Look for catch reports and match results, these will often highlight productive areas. Search for comments and questions naming the water in online forums and chat rooms. Search social media and join relevant groups. Walk around the water, speak to people fishing, find the bailiff and have a chat with him.

On any stillwater the fish will have a seasonal pattern to their movements. Some parts of a lake will be better in the summer, other parts will hold more fish in the winter.

Whilst doing your research, keep in mind any seasonal fish movements and hot spots. Although all this research will not be able to pinpoint a peg for every occasion, it should at least give you a rough area, a starting point.

Alternatively, you could just turn up and fish from a popular peg. A peg where the bank is worn with use, one which is peppered with bank stick and umbrella holes. Popular pegs should not be sniffed at, they are popular for a reason, even if that reason is that they are close to the car park. Either way, many anglers will put bait into the lake from a popular peg, the fish learn this and will see it as a reliable place of plenty.

A practical approach

The sort of waters we are interested in rarely have much in the way of obvious fish holding features to cast to. Instead we depend on the lake bed geography to hold features which may indicate where to cast.

Plumb the depths with a bomb as described in the Basic Skills section. Look out for any sudden changes in depth. Note any shelves or snags which might be a problem. Discover how quickly the depth changes and finally determine the nature of the bottom.

Reservoirs and gravel pits can dramatically increase in depth over a few metres. It is not always a good idea to fish just beyond a sudden drop off, as playing a fish over the edge is difficult and can cut the line. Ideally, the bottom will drop away at a sensible pace and flatten out at it's deepest point. Cast around with the bomb and find a couple of lines that have a firm bottom with no weeds or snags.

Setup for two swims

It is extremely difficult to know exactly where the fish will be, both in distance from the bank and in depth. Opening more than one swim is the best way to improve the odds. Two swims is usually enough, although some anglers will open, feed and rotate between as many as four. To cover both distance and depth, open one close swim in shallow water and one more distant swim in deep water which should suffice on most days.

Use a bomb to find a suitable area at between 20 and 30 metres for the short swim and another spot at 40 or 50 metres out for the long. To prevent spooking fish in the close swim when reeling in, ensure the swims are offset from each other. The last thing you want to happen is for a heavy, long range feeder rig to drag through the close swim on every retrieval. But don't have the swim so offset that you have to change the position of the front rod rest every time you switch swims. Arrange them to not interfere with each other, but still be in line enough to avoid constant faffing with the rod rests.

Swim 1

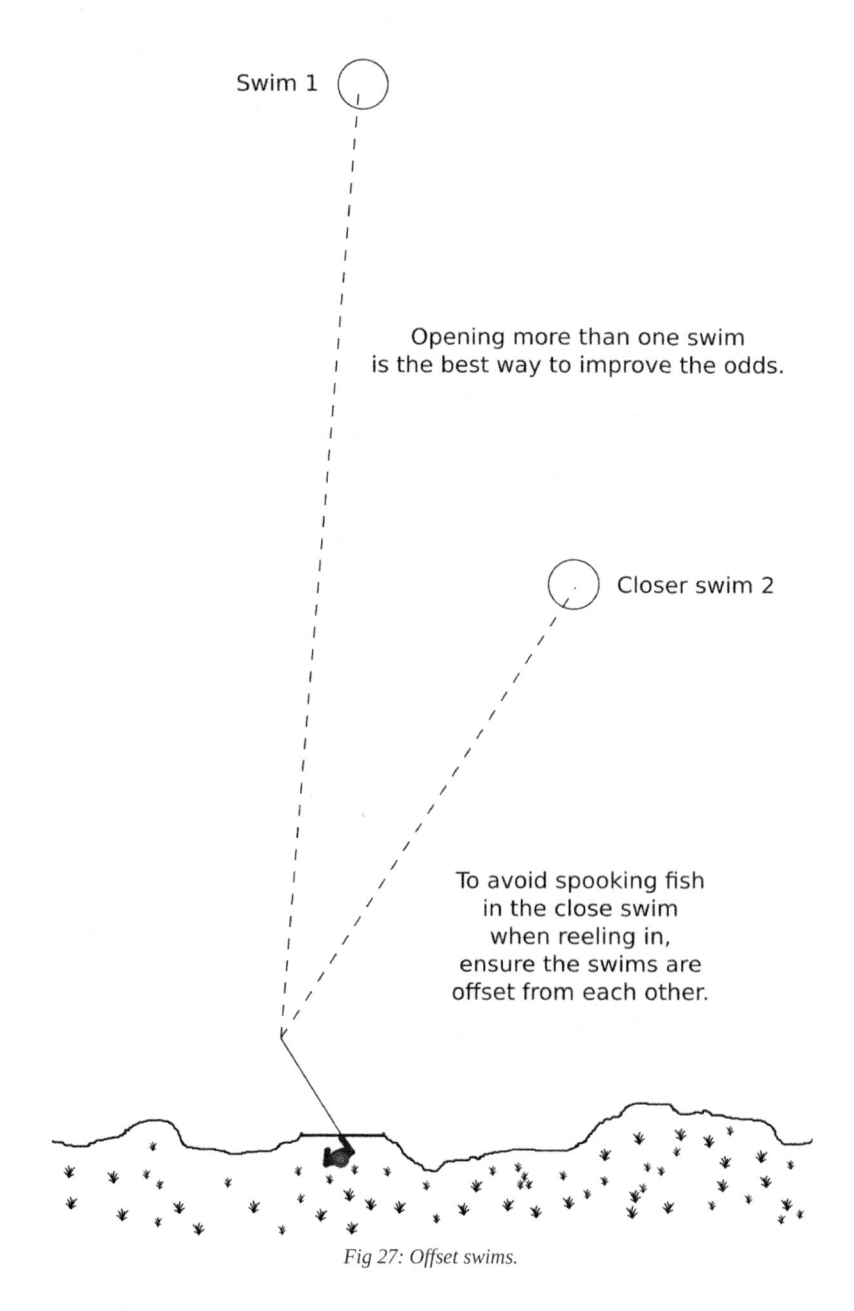

Opening more than one swim
is the best way to improve the odds.

Closer swim 2

To avoid spooking fish
in the close swim
when reeling in,
ensure the swims are
offset from each other.

Fig 27: Offset swims.

Rods and tips

Fishing two swims is a lot easier if you are lucky enough to own two feeder rods. A 12" rod using braid with a shock leader for the long line and a 10" with mono right through for the short. Rod and mainline selection is fairly easy as they are related to casting weight and distance. Selecting the correct strength of tip is less clear, but very important as using the wrong tip will definitely result in fewer fish. Unlike Carp fishing with a flatbed feeder where the fish self hook and virtually pull the rod in. Feeder fishing for silvers is more about interpreting the tips movements, reading bites and picking the rod up at the right time. This is not possible if the tip is wrong.

Quiver tips

Quiver tips are made of either glass fibre or carbon fibre. Glass fibre tips can be identified by their white colour at the exposed bottom end, whereas carbon tips are dark grey or black. Glass tips are very flexible and have a soft springy action. Carbon tips are stiffer and less forgiving. All tips are rated by their test curve, which is how much weight in ounces is needed to bend one to 90° angle.

Most feeder rods come with two or three different strength tips for use in different conditions. Deciding which tip to use can be a cause of hesitation and indecision for an angler. These feelings can give rise to doubts and a drop in confidence, neither of which helps us to catch fish and enjoy the day.

90°

Quiver tip test curve.
Measured by how much
weight in ounces is needed
to bend to a 90° angle.

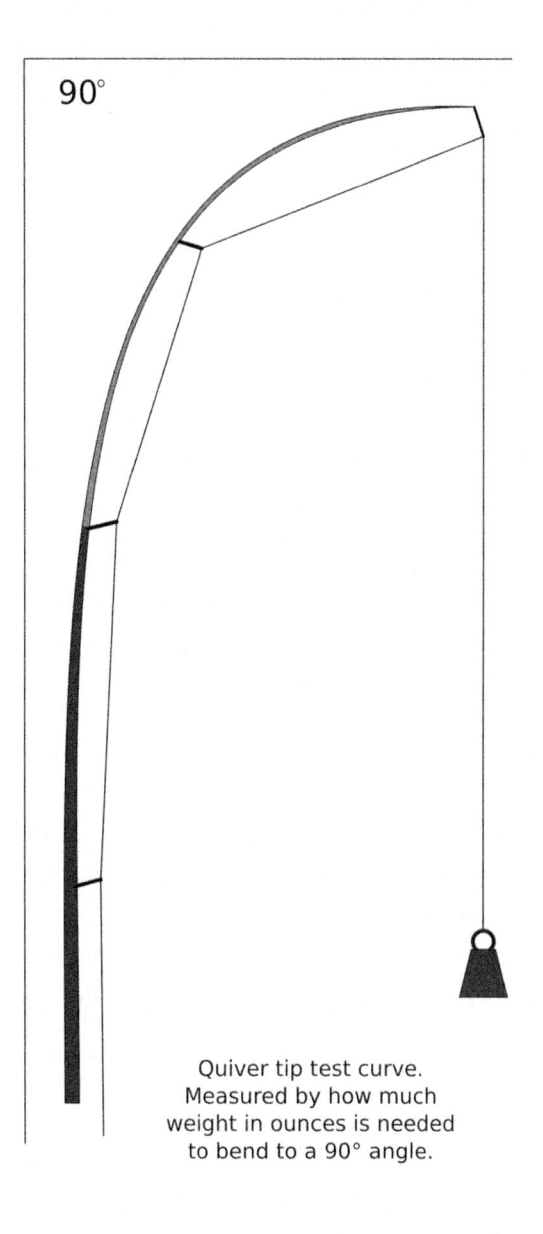

Fig 28: Quiver tip test curve.

The problem is that tip selection depends on a number of factors including the weather, flow or movement of the water, distance cast and fishing line used. Each of these factors combine to affect how a tip behaves and how well it signals a bite.

On a calm day, a soft 1oz tip will behave and report bites accurately from a line 40m away. But, if the wind starts to blow and the water begins to move, an undertow along with surface drift will result. A circulation in the water will begin causing a flow which will in turn push against all the submerged line. Pressure on the line will pull on the 1oz tip causing it to bend further, possibly to a point where it can no longer indicate a bite. The more distant the swim, the more line in the water, the greater the effect. The answer is to use a stiffer tip to compensate for the movement in the water.

Flow of water across the line can not be regarded as a constant. Using a braided main line which is much thinner than nylon in the same conditions, would pull much less on the tip, once more allowing the use of a softer tip. You can see why people get confused over which quiver tip to use, but there is an easy solution.

Trying to weigh up all the variables that can affect the tip is virtually impossible. Much better to assess the result and be guided by that. After plumbing the depth with a bomb and before attaching the rig. Cast to the swim and put the rod in the rod rests, tighten up as usual and wait. Finish setting up and come back to the rod a few minutes later to see where the tip has settled. If the flow or under tow have pulled the rod tip round too far then change the tip for a stiffer one.

If the tip has remained exactly where you set it, a softer tip might be possible.

In very calm conditions a soft tip is the first choice, but if there is any wind, or if you are fishing at distance, a stiffer tip will be needed. Use how the tip reacts to decide whether it is the right one or not. Remember, don't worry about the causes, just see the effect.

To show both drop back and pull bites, the tip should be at rest with a slight bend, the line is then under a small amount of tension to the rig. Any movement of the weight, or pull on the hook link will show at the tip. In dead calm conditions it may be necessary to tighten down to the feeder to put a slight bend in the tip. An offset from dead straight of one inch is enough. Wind powered movement in the water can also be enough on it's own to pull the tip an inch, which raises another interesting possibility. Imagine if you will, it's a windy day and with the rod in the rests the tow of the water pulls the tip two inches off straight. Two inches is not too bad, but will reduce sensitivity just a little. Changing to a stiffer tip may be too much, so to balance the setup, let some line out. Within seconds the tow will take up the slack and push it into a slight bow from tip to weight. The tip is now partly pulling against the weight and partly against the lesser pull on the line. By adjusting the amount of slack let into the line, very precise control can be exercised over how much of a bend is in the tip. This trick is called fishing the bow in river fishing, something we will look at later, but can be applied to stillwaters as well in the right conditions.

As a rough guide, glass fibre tips with test curves from ¼oz to 1oz are used to detect the shy, delicate bites of Roach, Skimmers and other silvers at close range. Carbon tips come in a much wider range from 1oz to as much as 6oz and cover all other feeder fishing conditions including rivers. Generally though, carbon tips of 1oz, 1½oz, 2oz and occasionally 3oz, will serve 99% of all other feeder fishing on lakes and reservoirs.

Feeding approach

There was a time, years ago, when the accepted wisdom of Bream fishing was to pile in a whole load of bait. This was done some hours before fishing to attract and hold a shoal ready for the angler. This idea works, or at least it does in some places. Bream that do not see much bait can be captivated and occupied for hours when they find a pile of free food. Nowadays, fishing is so popular that only the most exclusive waters escape the attention of the angling multitude. In my opinion, the days of prebaiting and piling in are for the most part gone. All fish including Bream, are well aware of anglers bait. With so many anglers putting bait in every day, the novelty of finding a big pile of free food is lost, in fact, it may serve as a warning of danger. Despite this, starting the day by introducing a small amount of feed is now the accepted wisdom.

An opening gambit of a few feeders full of groundbait and feed are enough to kick start a swim. Bream and Roach can be very fickle in their feeding habits. The type and quantity of feed included within the feeder can have a big effect on how the fish react.

An educated guess has to be made at the start of each session as to the best way to begin. The time of year and the desired species are perhaps the two most important factors.

The four seasons give us the broad brush strokes of feeding tactics. In winter the fish are least active and least likely to feed, so don't give them too much. At the other extreme, especially early summer before it gets stupidly hot, the fish are actively feeding, more feed will be needed.

Spring is always a good time of year. Fish will actively be on the lookout for anything they can eat. Temperatures can fluctuate wildly with sudden cold snaps and night frosts putting the brakes on a fish's activity. Autumn too has very changeable weather, but in a different way. In autumn the fish are preparing for the oncoming cold and scarcity of natural food, the opposite to spring. It makes me think that good quality bait is perhaps more important in autumn than at other times.

Doing your homework if you are new to fishing, or trying a fishery for the first time, can be an enormous help with your initial approach. Having an idea which species a water has a reputation for and from match reports, where hot spots are, will at least narrow down your options. The time of year and current weather conditions also indicate the mood of the fish. Just like us, there is weather they prefer and weather they don't. A little thought and some observation from the bank should be enough to offer clues as to an opening tactic.

One thing I like to do is dip my fingers in the water to "feel" the temperature. In the winter the water can feel painfully cold.

At these temperatures for me to imagine the fish would be interested in a good feed is optimistic beyond reason. No, this is a time to feed negatively, cautiously and hope to get a few bites.

Cold days

When the water is very cold, introducing too much feed will kill the swim. The fish will either eat their fill in the first few minutes or be put off by the barrage. One or two medium sized feeders filled with finely ground black or dark groundbait, which contains as little as four dead pinkies, is maybe all you can risk. On the first cast after the opening feed, once again literally containing only four pinkies. Bait the hook with a live maggot then watch and wait, looking for any signs of life. With luck you might see a line bite or two, maybe even catch a fish. If you don't after 30 minutes, a rethink is in order. Reel in and carefully check the maggot on the hook. If it appears chewed, flattened, or had it's innards sucked out, you can safely assume a fish has done this without your knowledge. This is why using a live maggot is so useful, they can show the presence of fish even when nothing else gives the slightest hint.

From this evidence, one fish at least is in the swim and peckish, but it did not give itself away. Shortening the hook link, giving the fish less room to move, should improve bite registration. Reload, recast and try again.

If after half an hour nothing has happened and the maggot comes back intact, a decision has to be made, try again or switch to the second swim.

An important difference between swims should be depth, make sure this is the case if you can. In winter, large bodies of deep water will stratify. In other words, separate into layers of water at different temperatures.

At the surface we found the water to be freezing cold, but this layer of cold water is on top and in contact with the air. Lower down in the water column will be a layer that is slightly warmer where the fish might be. By having two swims of different depths, one of them might be at a depth the fish find most comfortable. In this instance on a very cold day, I am tempted to try the second swim. I would not abandon the first swim, but keep it topped up with a couple of full feeders and a few pieces of feed at least every hour.

Hopefully, one of the two swims will contain some fish willing to feed, which moves us on to keeping them interested long enough to catch some of them. A pattern of regular feeding has to be one that keeps them coming, but over feeding is a real possibility on cold days.

Time how long it takes for a bite to happen. If bites are coming quickly, let's say in under three minutes, it's probably safe to assume there are a few fish in the swim which may require a steady supply of feed to keep them interested. Increasing the quantity and type of feed, perhaps a few dead red maggots or some chopped sweetcorn might be in order. Use the clues the fish give you to judge how much feed will keep them coming.

On days where a steady stream of Roach, skimmers and perhaps Perch are landed, try a bigger bait to see if any better fish are in the swim.

Double worm, four maggots, double caster, a grain of corn or a cocktail bait of a worm topped off with a pinky perhaps. If there are better fish there a bigger bait might bring them out.

What to do if the swim dies. Go back to a single maggot hook bait and maintain regular casting. On every retrieval check the maggot for damage and watch for line bites while in the water. If fish are still there, alter the presentation. Try different baits, change the hook link length, cast out with an empty feeder to cut back on the feed. If all else fails, try more feed in the feeder in the hope that under feeding is the problem. Finally change to the other swim and see if the fish are there and if they are, start the whole process again.

Mild days

In the spring and autumn there will be days when I put my fingers in the water and find it to have no temperature. Of course in reality it does, it's just that it is not noticeably cold or hot, tepid I supposed you could say. These are the sort of days when normal people are seen cutting the grass, decorating the house and performing the most hateful of all tasks; washing the car! The temperature is ideal to perform these tedious tasks without shivering with cold or sweating like a pig, usefully comfortable weather. At all costs avoid playing a character in this idyllic domestic picture, as temperate days are fishing days.

The weather touching the surface of the water is no longer trying to freeze it. No longer is there a great difference between the temperature at the surface and that deeper down, the strata have gone.

Mixing of water from different layers can now happen powered by the wind causing surface movement and undertow. Unless the water is extremely deep, a large fishery will be at a fairly uniform temperature.

A shallow fishery is more susceptible to the whim of our environment of air and sun, but here too the water will be tepid and the fish happy. Time to forget the negative cautious approach we laboured under scratching around for a few bites in the cold. Now we can knuckle down and work to catch a good few fish with a positive approach.

A two swim approach as always, one close and one distant. Both swims can be fed generously with a rich mix consisting of groundbait and a selection of feed particles. When fish are actively feeding because of favourable conditions, neat fishmeal groundbait may not be necessary. A 50/50 mix of groundbait and brown bread crumb will do the job just as well. For the initial feeding use a second working bowl to make up a special mix to kick start the swims.

An example might be:

1 part fishmeal groundbait
1 part brown breadcrumb
2 parts soaked micro pellets
1 part casters
1 part dead red maggots

Sprinkling of sweetcorn or hemp seeds or both.

This is a rich combination of baits made from components known to work, none of these are novel or experimental. Use this mix on both swims, cast six large feeders full to each. Put any leftover feed to one side for later.

Fill the primary working bowl with a 50/50 mix of fishmeal and brown crumb groundbait, no micro pellets. Drop a few dead maggots and casters in the bowl and scoop them up into the feeder and begin fishing.

Try to match the amount of feed introduced to balance the number of fish suspected in the swim, while simultaneously promoting some competition between the fish. One of the problems with the old idea of filling in with bait, is the fact that with so much bait spread out on the bottom, the probability of a fish finding the hookbait is greatly reduced. Use enough bait, but not too much is the key.

Initially expect to catch small Roach or Skimmers as small fish are always the first to turn up to a free meal. Keep a close eye on how the fish respond to the feed introduced. Watch the quiver tip not only for proper bites, but also for line bites which can be very revealing. A slow Steady pull on the tip which suddenly springs back can be a sign of bigger fish in the swim.

Keep feeding the swim on every cast and hopefully in time some better fish will push out the small ones. Changing to a bigger hookbait can weed out the small fish proving the better fish have arrived. Just to clarify, a bigger bait can mean several maggots, a worm, or a cocktail, not just one big bait.

If evidence suggests fish are in the swim, but not taking the bait, change something. Please, Please don't just sit and hope, take action. Change the hookbait, up the feed or reduce the feed. Try a different size of hook or diameter of hook link. Moving the feeder will often result in a bite. Lift the rod an inch or two off the rod rest and pull the feeder a foot along the bottom. Place the rod back down and tighten up. Ring the changes until you discover what it is the fish want on the day.

One of the best things to try is chopped worm. In a small pot, chop some worms up with multi blade worm scissors. Include them in the feeder as you would any other feed, they can be combined with dead reds or casters or used on their own. Some anglers swear by them and will use them very regularly through a session. Chopped worms in the feed demand worms on the hook. The tail of a lob worm or a couple of Dendrobaenas tipped with a pinky or caster can often cause an instant response from a swim that seems void of any fish.

If chopped worms fail, kick start the swim once again with four feeders of the initial mix from the secondary working bowl. Change to the other swim and let the first one rest for an hour or so.

Temperate days of spring are often the very best times to go fishing. The fish are hungry after the winter and their natural food has yet to flourish. These days are not always the most comfortable for humans though, many people don't go fishing until the weather is comfortable for them. Those long lazy summer days when the sun doesn't set until bedtime and goose bumps never appear.

The days when every peg on the water is occupied with the hopeful, who watch and long for one of those big fish cruising in plain sight at the surface, but then go home at tea time.

Hot days

I'm not one for early mornings, you won't find me creeping about at 3am trying to load the car in silence. Neither will you find me on the bank in the heat of the day. Mid afternoon into the evening is when I like to fish on a hot day. Many people who have been there since dawn, or who have baked in the midday sun, head home for tea just as I arrive. By seven in the evening I often have the place to myself. The evening stillness and peace descend, every noise, every ripple and every sign of fish can be clearly seen on a calm summer evening. What could be better.

It is surprising when arriving on the bank hot and bothered from carrying my gear, the water feels warm to my already hot hands. A layer of warm water has developed in the high summer sun like a blanket over the lake. In the winter a layer of cold water, perhaps with a lid of ice develops trapping warmer water beneath. During the two weeks of summer we get here in England, a blanket of warm water develops on the surface which traps cooler water beneath it. Separate strata's of warm water at the surface to cool water at the bottom, will develop in deep lakes. Shallow lakes may still have a warm top layer, but lack the cooler water in the absence of any depths. Shallow lakes really are at the mercy of the weather.

On cold and mild days the subject of oxygen in the water never really arises, but as water gets warmer it holds less and less oxygen. A spell of hot weather can see oxygen levels drop, which will distress the fish and put them off the feed. In extreme cases some fish might not survive. This is why many fisheries ban keepnets and limit the amount of bait an angler is allowed to introduce.

Another event that will put the fish down is a summer storm. The sudden drop in air pressure literally sucks the oxygen out of the water, plus the rain can put the fish off for the rest of the day. Assume sudden changes in weather conditions at any time of year can affect the fishing, something to remember when deciding how much to feed.

If you are a morning person, being on the bank at sunrise is probably the best plan for a good summer session. Feed two swims, one deep and one shallow, or one close or one distant if the venue is generally shallow. I might be tempted to include micro pellets in the initial feed on a morning assault if there is a choice of depth, but leave them out on a lake with uniform depth where the fish have no choice but to endure the conditions.

As the seasons pass and your local knowledge of a fishery increases, quantities, patterns and feeding tactics will improve. In time you will become the local guy who knows all there is to know about a place. How long will this take? I would say five seasons, which sounds a long time, but it soon passes.

Feeding the swim is the next most important aspect of angling after location. A combination of faith in the bait you use, observation and common sense will see you clear to catching fish more often than not. Feeding is a skill which takes time to cultivate and understand, but it is well worth the effort. It is the one thing all good anglers have a feel for. If you are satisfied with your results one trip in five, consider yourself a good angler.

River feeder fishing

Out of all the species of interest Roach are the most widespread in a river. They can be found everywhere except in the streamy upper reaches and the lower tidal stretches. Bream prefer the lowland areas, the deep, wide slow moving sections, as do most of the other common species.

Lowland sections meander through flood plains. The water is slow moving and can come to near standstill in a dry summer. Fine sediment covers the river bed with submerged weeds and marginal weeds are common which Bream use for spawning. These areas also sustain vast numbers of invertebrates and other natural food appealing to all fish. The water is often coloured which gives fish more confidence when feeding.

River setup

Apart from the presence of a slow flow, fishing a lowland section of river is remarkably similar to fishing a lake. The same rods, reels and rigs can be used, one only has to account for the flow.

Casting distances tend to be much shorter and the slow flow in the lowlands only requires light weight feeders. A chosen feeder only needs to be heavy enough to hold the bottom.

Many anglers position their rod pointing up in front of them to keep as much line out of the flow as possible. This might only be necessary when fishing a stronger flow, for the most part the rod can be as low down as it would be fishing a lake.

Having the rod high can produce too many line bites as it cuts through the feeding fish rather than staying close to the bottom out of the way.

Cast around with a bomb to test depth and feel the bottom. Locate an area of clean river bed devoid of any submerged weed or snags, ideally a Bream filled deeper part. If there are no deep areas, then a clean area of the river bed will do fine.

Anglers have developed many river feeder rigs over the years, but they are often just variations of the simple running rig. Fixed rigs, especially fixed paternoster rigs, had a big following at one time, but for fish safety reasons they are not as popular as they once were. I only use one rig these days and that is a standard running rig, this simple rig is perfectly fine for the parts of the river we are most interested in.

Feeder weight and quiver tips

Every piece of tackle from reel to hook should compliment and balance one another. With most casts being less than 30m, an 11ft rod paired with a 4000 reel loaded with 6lb line will suffice.

There may be occasion to use heavier equipment if fishing a wide tidal stretch, but on the whole fairly light tackle will do.

Tie the running rig and attach a feeder to the line. Cast out and feather the line down, trapping it under your finger as the feeder hits the surface. Wait for the tip to spring straight when the feeder lands on the river bed. Put the line behind the line clip to set the casting distance. Make another cast or two, hitting the clip with the rod upright to ensure the distance set is correct.
Stopping the feeder with the rod upright will cause a little slack line between rod and feeder, which is correct and useful.

Hold the rod still or set it down in the rests and watch the tip. After a few seconds the flow will take up the slack in the line both sinking it and tightening it up to the quiver tip. If the tip is pulled round too far by the current it is too weak, it needs to be replaced with a stiffer tip. Conversely, if the tip remains straight a softer tip will be better. If the tip bounces back and forth, the feeder is being pushed along the bottom in the flow. Or more accurately, the force of water against all the line in the water between rod tip and feeder is enough to dislodge the feeder.

Increase the weight of the feeder until it is just heavy enough to hold the bottom, but don't overdo it. Use the lightest feeder possible.

Fishing the bow

Water flowing downstream past the submerged line between the water surface and the feeder, creates pull on the line which can overcome the weight of the feeder dislodging it from the river bed. A balance needs to be struck between the weight of the feeder, the flow of the water past the line and the pull from the tip. In a perfect setup, the feeder needs only to be just heavy enough to hold position, with all the forces involved balanced. The slightest additional pull from a fish will dislodge the feeder causing a bite at the tip. Usually a drop back followed by a proper pull. The drop back is caused by the feeder moving suddenly releasing the line. The following pull is caused by the sudden movement of the feeder jerking against the hook link and pricking the fish's mouth.

To create this critical balance, as it turns out, is quite simple. Begin by guessing the stiffness of the tip and the weight of the feeder needed for the conditions. Cast to your chosen spot and wait for the feeder to touch down on the bottom. Put the rod in the rests and wait for the flow to tighten the line. Look at the tip to see if it needs changing. If the tip looks fine but the feeder is being dragged along the bottom, pull some line off the reel using the distance between the spool and the first rod ring as a guide. If after three pulls of line from reel to ring the feeder is still being dragged downstream, a heavier feeder is definitely required. Change the feeder and try again. Keep adding weight until just one or one and a half pulls puts enough slack in the line to stop the feeder moving. By balancing the slackness in the line against the weight of the feeder, a very sensitive setup can be made.

I appreciate all this seems a bit of a faff when a heavier feeder will do the trick, but a heavier feeder will definitely reduce the number of bites you see.

By "fishing the bow" using a balanced setup, the feeder almost becomes weightless and easy for an unwitting fish to disturb. Fishing the bow also allows the use of lighter feeders than normal in a strong flow.

Keep it simple on a river

Feeding river fish is basically the same as feeding fish that inhabit a lake. They love maggots, casters and worms, but will also eat sweetcorn, hemp and pellets. The seasons, changes in water temperature and oxygen levels all affect river fish in the same way as lake fish.

No surprises when I say feed a swim less in the winter than summer. Use fine groundbaits with little food content in the winter and rich mixes in the summer. Essentially the principles outlined fishing a lake apply just as well on a river, what is different is how they are applied.

The first rule of fishing a river is to keep everything plain and simple. Unless the river is very popular or used for matches, it is safe to say many of the fish have never seen an angler. Technical rigs and man made baits are just not needed to catch river Bream, skimmers, Roach and the other common river species.

The same basic running rig for lakes is ideal for river fishing. Personally I don't use any other rig, not even the feeder link running rig. Please don't be tempted to add additional swivels, beads or other bits because all that happens is small fish try to eat them causing false bites.

To get the bait to the bottom, use either a cage feeder or a plastic feeder, depending on depth and flow. Keep everything natural and simple.

Maggot feeder

More often than not, the water of a lowland river will carry some colour. In these conditions a plastic feeder or cage feeder is used to carry groundbait and feed to the fish. The groundbait acts as the medium to carry the feed, while the river carries the taste and flavours of the groundbait downstream which can attract the fish to the bait.

After a calm spell of weather, winter or summer, all the colour can drop out of the water leaving it crystal clear. Although the usual groundbait feeder approach can still work, a maggot feeder can often be even better, because the fish can see the maggots in the clear water.

Maggot feeders have a cap at either end of a tube which has holes through which maggots can escape. A small hook tied to a long hook link attached to a running rig is the usual setup. Fish over a clear section of river bed where the maggots can be seen wriggling around. Make regular casts to keep maggots going in and build up a swim.

Small Roach or Perch are likely to be the first on the scene, hopefully followed by better fish later in the session. There is no secret to this style of fishing. So long as the water is clear enough for the fish to use their sight to hunt, and regular casts keep the feed coming, you will catch.

Bread

Bread is a bait that for some reason fish immediately know is food. Like worms and maggots, bread is universally liked by river fish. Winter is perhaps the best time to fish with bread, but it works well in summer too.

The usual setup is once again a long hook link attached to the faithful running rig and a cage feeder. The cage feeder is filled with slightly dampened white bread crumbs with a pinch of bread flake on a size 14 hook.

As the feeder sinks to the bottom, particles of bread crumb escape and attractively drift downstream. Most of the crumb should remain in the feeder down to the river bed, where it swells and comes out of the feeder. The crumb will spread downstream creating a cloud of particles and an eye catching white area on the bottom. Just like the maggot feeder, bread is a visual bait and needs clear water for the best results.

A piece of flake pinched on to the shank of the hook, will fall slowly through the water settling gently on the bottom. Fish often intercept the flake on the way down, producing an almost instant bite. Repeated casts will pull fish down from the upper layers closer to the river bed, bringing them together over the area we want to catch them.

The fishing can get very hectic once the fish switch onto bread. On a good day there won't be time to put the rod in the rests before another fish is pulling the tip!

List of feeders

Plastic open end feeder

For rivers and deep still waters

Feed is held inside the feeder by a plug of groundbait at each end. Once in the water the groundbait breaks down releasing the feed bait within.

Primarily designed for running water, the open end plastic feeder deposits it's payload of feed close to the hook bait. The hook link should be set so the feed washes down around the hook bait. On a slow river the hook link may be as short as eight inches, but in a faster flow it could be two or more feet.

Use with Running rig or feeder link running rig.

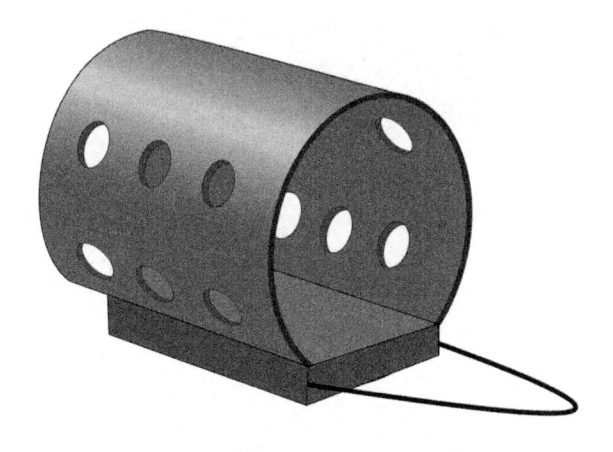

Fig 29: Plastic open end feeder.

Cage feeder
Still water and slow rivers

The wide open mesh of a cage feeder allows feed to quickly escape. Use with groundbait or liquidised bread with or without feed particles. A dry mix will quickly explode from the feeder once in the water. The feed may wash out as the feeder sinks, but they can be used in water up to six feet deep with the right mix of feed.

Use with Running rig or feeder link running rig
Inline versions available.

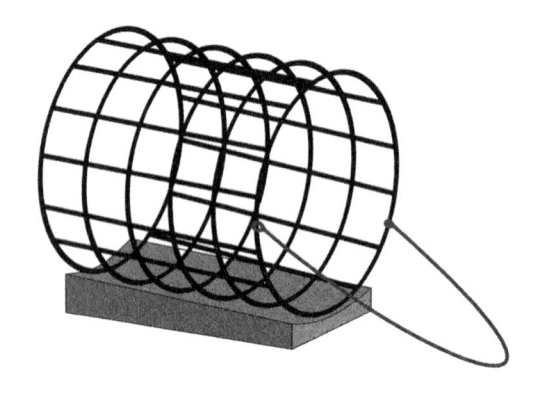

Fig 30: Cage feeder.

Rocket feeder
Still water

Rocket feeders are designed to increase the distance and accuracy of casting. In a headwind or crosswind, the aerodynamic weight forward design allows the feeder to cut through the air more easily. The helicopter rig is an ideal setup for maximum tangle free distance casting.

Rockets come in both cage and plastic styles. In water of over 2m, the more enclosed plastic rocket feeders will hold the feed in right to the bottom. The wire cage variety is better in shallow water.

Use with Helicopter rig.

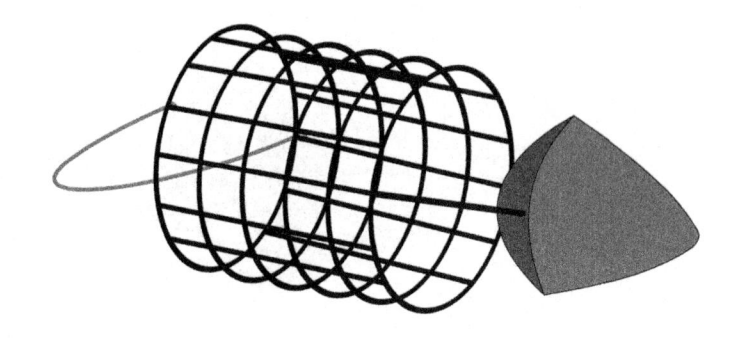

Fig 31: Rocket feeder.

Maggot feeder
River and still water

Open one end and pack the feeder with maggots. Once in the water, maggots escape through the holes attracting fish to your swim. On a slow river the hook link may be as short as eight inches, but in a faster flow it could be two or more feet. Maggot feeders can be used with a long hook link to fish on the drop in still water, which is a very effective way of catching Roach and Rudd.

Use with Running rig, inline versions available.

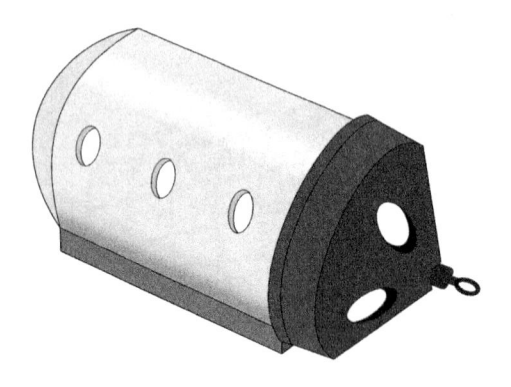

Fig 32: Maggot feeder.

Dome feeder

Large still waters

The dome feeder is used to carry a good quantity of bait. Most useful on big waters that support large roving shoals of fish. When the fish pass through the swim they can very quickly clear it of any existing bait. Dome feeders can top up with a good amount of feed on each cast and may hold the fish longer.

Fill the dome with feed and cap off with groundbait. Wait a minute after casting in for the groundbait to break down, then move the feeder a few inches to empty.

The dome feeder works best on big waters with no features. Use the feeder to create a feature of free offerings to stop and hold passing shoals of fish.

Use with Running rig.

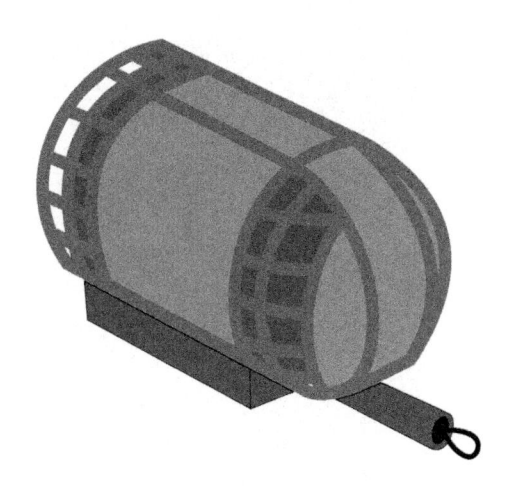

Fig 33: Dome feeder.

Bell feeder
Large deep still waters

The Bell feeder can carry a reasonable amount of bait on each cast. It has a more enclosed design than the dome feeder making it more suited to holding the bait in to reach the bottom of a deep water swim.

Fill the bell with feed and cap off with groundbait. Wait a minute after casting in for the groundbait to break down, then move the feeder a few inches to empty and straighten the hook link.

Use with Running rig or Helicopter rig.

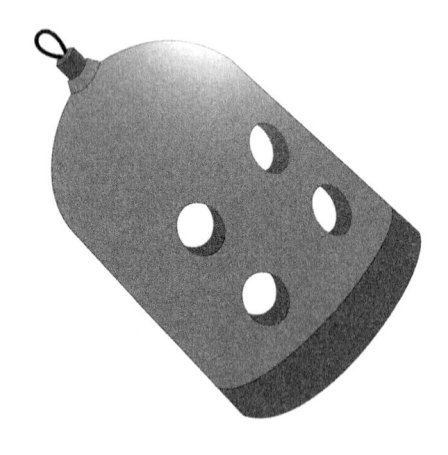

Fig 34: Bell feeder.

Window feeder

Big natural waters

Window feeders are designed for accurate long distance casting. Their aerodynamic slim weight forward bodies cleanly cut through wind for maximum distance.

Scoop feed into the feeder through the side window and cap off with groundbait. The larger window feeders can carry a lot of bait making them ideal to kick start the swim or feed a shoal of hungry Bream.

The groundbait will quickly break down in the water, but the feed will not fully empty from the feeder until it is retrieved for reloading.

Use with Helicopter rig.

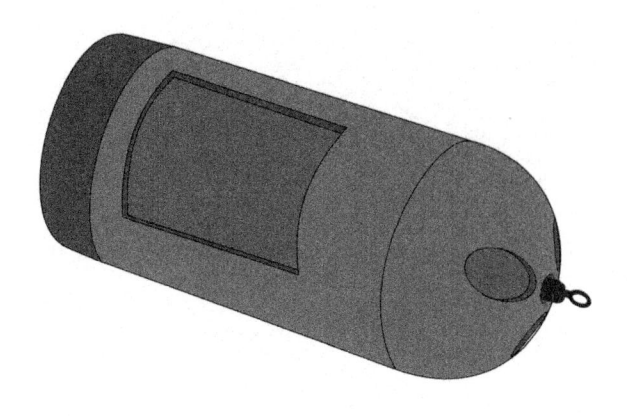

Fig 35: Window feeder.

Finned feeder
Still waters with silty bottom

The finned feeder is simply a plastic feeder with a fin on either side. The fins slow the feeder on it's descent to the lake bed for a soft landing on silt. The fins also help the feeder lift off the bottom very quickly.

Use the finned feeder on silty bottomed still waters in the same way as a plastic feeder.

Use with Running rig.

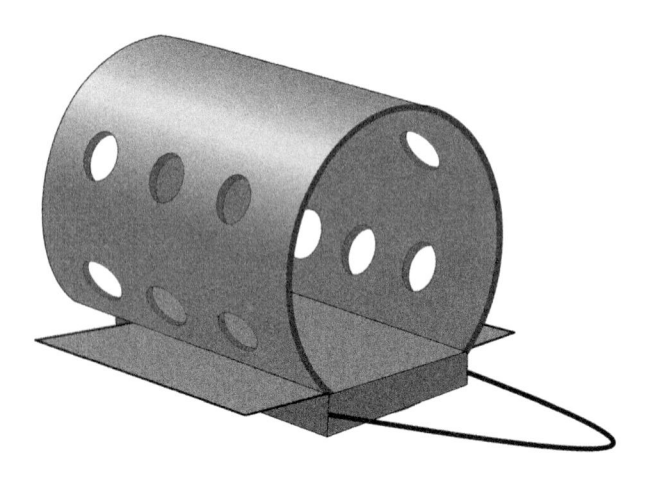

Fig 36: Finned plastic feeder.

Further thoughts

I have been giving some thought to the subject of dissolved oxygen in water and how it affects the fish. We know water temperature has a big effect on how active fish are and how much food they need to eat. Cold conditions slow them down and reduce their appetite. Warm conditions favour our native fish, but a heatwave can put them off.

The amount of oxygen dissolved in water also changes with temperature. Cold water can hold much more oxygen than warm. As the temperature rises, dissolved oxygen decreases and at some point the fish become uncomfortable and go off the feed.

I said earlier that the spring is the best time to go fishing, dissolved oxygen may play a part in this. From May to June, the weather is getting warmer slowly raising the water temperature as it does. I believe that in spring, not only are the fish hungry after winter, but the water temperature and oxygen levels hit an ideal balance for the fish.

Later in the year as the weather gets warmer, not only does the oxygen level drop, but there is also an abundance of natural food, the fish have plenty to eat.

When a heatwave develops, water temperatures at the surface can reach 25°C or more causing a sudden drop in dissolved oxygen. If we have a summer storm, the accompanying low pressure system can literally suck oxygen out of a lake, suddenly dropping the oxygen levels still further.

Observing and noting these changes in temperature and air pressure can help in deciding where to fish and importantly how much to feed. After location, how a swim is fed, is the most important factor determining how many fish will be caught.

A lake with good oxygen levels will often look bright, sparkly and have a slight green tinge, so I assume the fish will be in the mood for food. If the water is dull brown or grey, I suspect low oxygen levels and apathetic fish, I cut the feed right back and fish for bites.

I am sure oxygen levels play a part in how well the fish receive bait, but at this time it is for me unsubstantiated. I added it to the end of the book simply as food for thought, I hope you found it interesting.

Best of luck with your fishing.